The MAILBOX The Education Center®

STO

FRIENDS OF ACPL

Social Studies

OF MAILBOX® MAGAZINE

Grades 4–5

D1200010

The best social studies activities and reproducibles from the 1998–2002 issues of *The Mailbox®* magazine!

- **U.S. History**
- **Geography**
- **Latin America**
- **State Activities**
- **Canada**
- **Citizenship**

And many more social studies topics!

Editorial Team: Becky S. Andrews, Kimberley Bruck, Karen P. Shelton, Diane Badden, Thad H. McLaurin, Debra Liverman, Karen A. Brudnak, Sarah Hamblet, Hope Rodgers, Dorothy C. McKinney

Production Team: Lisa K. Pitts, Pam Crane, Rebecca Saunders, Jennifer Tipton Cappoen, Chris Curry, Sarah Foreman, Theresa Lewis Goode, Clint Moore, Greg D. Rieves, Barry Slate, Donna K. Teal, Zane Williard, Tazmen Carlisle, Irene Harvley-Felder, Amy Kirtley-Hill, Kristy Parton, Cathy Edwards Simrell, Lynette Dickerson, Mark Rainey

www.themailbox.com

Table of Contents

Building Character

Building Character

Give Group Work a Hand!

Promote teamwork and cooperative learning in your classroom with this student-made bulletin board. Divide your class into six groups; then instruct each group to work together to trace the outline of each member's right and left hands. Photograph each group working together on this step. Next, have each student cut out and write his name on the front of his hand outlines. Collect the hand cutouts. After the film has been developed, have each group staple its hand cutouts in a circle around its photo on a bulletin board. Title the board "A Round of Applause for Our Group!" When groups change or new students are added to the class, simply move the hands into different circles and take additional pictures.

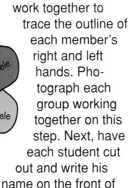

Terry Healy
Eugene Field Elementary
Manhattan, KS

Pat on the Back

Heighten students' self-esteem with this back-pattin' activity! Provide each student with a paper plate and two pieces of masking tape. Have the student trace his hand on the back side of the plate. Assist each student in taping his plate onto his back so that his "pat on the back" (handprint) is showing. Then have students give each other pats on the back by writing specific compliments on each other's plates. Encourage all students to sign all classmates' plates. Before allowing students to remove and read their plates, discuss what it feels like to give and receive compliments.

Kim Marinelli
La Barriere Crossings
Winnipeg, Manitoba, Canada

I Have Really Blossomed!

Plant a seed of self-esteem and watch students really grow with this end-of-the-year poetry writing activity. Have each student make a list of all the things she has learned or improved on throughout the year. Instruct the student to use her list to write a poem describing all of the ways she has blossomed this year. Take a picture of each student wearing a paper flower headpiece and a crepe paper stem that wraps around her body (see the illustration). Have the student share her picture and poem with her parent(s) at an end-of-the-year conference.

Betty J. Bowlin
Henry Elementary
Ballwin, MO

B.A.T.S.

Keep students from going batty when conflicts arise with this simple self-control strategy. Teach your class this four-step mnemonic device: *B*reathe; *A*sk yourself to count to ten; *T*hink of your favorite place; and *S*ay, "I'm okay; I can handle it!" Write this strategy on several bat cutouts. Then post the bats in various locations around the classroom. When a student is about to lose his self-control, point to a bat or say, "Bats!" The student, as instructed earlier, does the steps silently. Watch the number of problems decline as your students learn that there are other ways to handle conflicts.

Michele Raece
Maplewood Heights School, Renton, WA

Breathe.
Ask yourself to count to ten.
Think of your favorite place.
Say, "I'm okay; I can handle it!"

Wanted: Good Citizens

Build student character with this picture-perfect bulletin board. Take candid photos of six students in the act of being good citizens. Number each picture and post it on a bulletin board. Then write corresponding numbers on four or five index cards for each photo. Distribute one card to each student. Direct the student to explain on her card how the corresponding photo demonstrates good citizenship. Post each card around its photo. Repeat this process for several weeks until each student has been photographed.

Pat Twohey, Old County Road School
Smithfield, RI

What's So Special About...

Recognize students' attributes with this biweekly display. Randomly choose a student to honor. Have the student's classmates share aloud his special characteristics, making sure not to repeat a trait. Next, give each student a sheet of paper on which to write his comment. While the students are working, have the featured child draw a self-portrait. Display the self-portrait and positive comments on a bulletin board. After two weeks, send home the comments with a personal message of your own.

Marsha Schmus, Ypsilanti, MI

How Does Your Garden Grow?

Use the space below your board to let your students' positive thoughts blossom! When a student has something nice to say about a classmate or the class, have him trace a flower pattern onto construction paper, write his comment on the flower, cut it out, and attach a pipe cleaner stem and paper leaves. Have him "plant" (tape) his flower below the board. By the end of the year, your garden will be bursting with positive pats on the back!

Elizabeth Loeser, Jacksonville, FL

BUILDING Caring and Compassion

Help From a Fuzzy Friend

Students sometimes come to school needing a little extra compassion and empathy because of a family crisis, the illness or death of a loved one, or other stressful situations. Many times classmates have no clue about what the affected student is experiencing. Introduce a fuzzy little friend to help students understand more about compassion. Glue two wiggle eyes to a pom-pom. When a student is going through a difficult time, talk with him privately; then give him this fuzzy companion to keep on his desktop. Seeing this special friend atop a student's desk will signal classmates to be extra kind and considerate.

Julie Granchelli
Towne Elementary
Medina, NY

Character Trait T Charts

Help clarify students' understanding of the character trait of empathy with this easy activity. Discuss with students the meaning of *empathy*. Then draw a T chart on poster board as shown. Encourage students to help you fill in each side of the chart. Then display the poster in the classroom as a reminder of how students can demonstrate this important trait. Use this idea to explore other character traits, such as respect, responsibility, and honesty.

Irene Taylor
Bridgewater, NJ

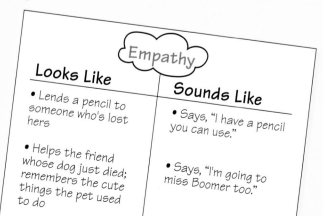

Empathy

Looks Like
• Lends a pencil to someone who's lost hers
• Helps the friend whose dog just died; remembers the cute things the pet used to do

Sounds Like
• Says, "I have a pencil you can use."
• Says, "I'm going to miss Boomer too."

Recuperation Rx

Have a student who'll be under the weather for a while? Use his absence as an opportunity for your students to show that they care. Tape two more than a class set of colorful, unlined index cards together top-to-bottom as shown. On the top card, write "[the number of students in your class] Things to Do While Recuperating." On the bottom card, write "We miss you. Get well soon!" Place the taped cards on a table along with a supply of colored pencils and markers. Have each student, in turn, come to the table to write and illustrate on a card something fun or corny that the absent child can do while he recuperates. Accordion-fold the cards into a stack; then send this class card to the sick child. Not only will this activity help your students understand more about caring, but it will let the recipient know just how much he's missed—and keep him busy too!

Adopt a Family

The holidays are perfect for teaching students about caring for others—especially if your class adopts a needy family! To find a family for this project, contact your local Family Services Department. Invite other classes at your grade level to participate so that each class can concentrate on a different family member. Spend the month of December collecting new and used toys, clothes, and other gifts for the family. To provide for students who may not be able to contribute to the collection, stress that an *idea* for a gift can be just as important as a contribution that costs money. If desired, also gather ingredients for a scrumptious holiday feast. What a wonderful way to get students thinking about *giving* at a time when receiving is uppermost in their minds!

Julia Alarie
Essex Middle School
Essex, VT

State Activities

Stellar State History Activities

What can a stellar teacher like you find in this star-studded collection? Plenty of all-star activities that investigate your state's history!

*with contributions by Dana Sanders
Cartersville, GA*

This place called Virginia sounds pretty cool.

Scout It Out!

Skills: Understanding the influence of geography on a state, thinking critically

Make students aware of geography's role in the development of your state with this fun group activity. First, announce that the class is an official colonial scouting party that has been hired by a European monarchy to explore your state and report back on its suitability for colonization. Next, divide the class into three (or six) groups. Assign one of the following topics about your state to each group: physical features, climate, valuable resources. Give each group several sheets of chart paper and markers. Then instruct it to research its topic and write its findings on the chart paper.

On the day groups are to present their findings, play the role of a monarch by wearing a paper crown and a large beach towel robe. Have each group present its findings to you and your court (the class). After the presentations, ask each student (or group) to write a letter to you giving his recommendations on the following:

- Should this area be colonized? Why or why not?
- What predictions can you make about life in this area?

What's in a Name?

Skill: Knowing the origins of important names of places in a state

There's a lot of history hidden in the names on your state's map. Bring that history out of hiding with this easy-to-do idea! First, help students brainstorm a list of simple songs with familiar tunes, such as "Row, Row, Row Your Boat" and "Jingle Bells." Write these song titles on the board. Next, display a large map of your state. Ask students to identify several cities, rivers, counties, and other places (monuments, tourist attractions, landforms, etc.) that your class has studied or read about. List these items on the board beside the previous list. Then divide the class into pairs and assign an item from this second list to each twosome. Instruct each pair to research its item to discover the origin of its name. Then challenge the duo to create a song—sung to a familiar tune from the first list—that can teach the class about the name's origin. Provide time for students to practice their songs before they present them to the class. If you have any extremely shy students, allow them to record their songs before class and play the recordings instead of performing live.

State History Time Capsule
**Skill: Evaluating the importance of major events
in a state's history**

Use the ready-to-go reproducible on page 11 to challenge your students to think critically about the major events in your state's history. Give each student a copy of page 11. After reading and discussing the introduction and steps as a class, have each student complete a copy of the page as directed. (If desired, let students complete Step 1 in pairs or small groups.) When students have finished the page, divide the class into small groups. Then have each student share his time capsule and letter with his group. If desired, have students cut out their time capsules to post with the letters on a bulletin board.

Historical Personalities Parade

**Skill: Understanding how the ideas of significant
people affected a state's history**

Who were the people who put your state on the map? Find out with an activity that results in a super student-made display! First, make a list of important people associated with your state's history. Have each student choose a person to research. Direct the student to find out about the person's main contributions to your state and the nation, his or her personal characteristics, and other interesting or unusual facts. After the student has taken her notes, have her pretend to be her famous person and write a first-person description. Direct the student to proofread her description and make any corrections or changes. Then have her copy the description onto white paper.

Next, provide each student with the materials listed below and guide her through the steps. Display the finished figures and speech bubbles in a hallway to create a parade of famous folks from your state. For another activity on studying your state's famous people, see "Where Would We Be Without You?" on page 13. *Julia Alarie, Essex Middle School, Essex, VT*

Materials: two 12" x 18" sheets of construction paper, pencil, ruler, scissors, glue, 9" x 12" sheet of white construction paper, crayons or markers

Steps:
1. Fold one larger sheet of construction paper in half lengthwise. Draw two straight lines on the folded paper as shown.
2. Cut along the lines, saving the scraps.
3. Unfold the upside-down V-shaped piece. This will be the torso and legs of your person.
4. Trim away the points of the two larger paper scraps. Then glue them to the back of the torso for arms.
5. Cut out a paper circle for the head. Also cut out hands and feet and any objects you'd like the person to hold. Add details with crayons or markers to make the model look like your famous person. Then glue the features to the torso.
6. Fold the arms forward to create different positions.
7. Trim the excess paper around your description. Then glue the description onto the white construction paper. Cut the construction paper into the shape of a conversation bubble.

A Penny for Your Thoughts

Skills: Understanding major events in a state's history, writing a description

Raid your loose-change jar for this "cents-ational" state history activity! Collect a penny for each student, trying to find a wide range of years. Also make a copy of page 12 for each student. Give each student her penny and her copy of page 12. Challenge the student to identify and research an important event in your state's history that occurred during the year that her penny was minted. Then ask her to write a description of the event on an index card and tape her penny to a corner of the card. After each student shares her description with the class, have her glue the card on one of her penny cutouts as shown. Then have her glue the cutouts back to back, sandwiching a length of yarn between them as shown. Suspend the coins from your ceiling for a shower of state history facts!

Scrambled Skits

Skills: Understanding major events in a state's history, writing a skit

Use this creative group activity to set the stage for a better understanding of key events in your state's history. Divide the class into groups and assign one important event in your state's history to each group. Then challenge each group to write a short skit that tells about its event. The catch? The group must include at least five errors about the event in its skit. Provide one class period for writing the skits and another for practicing them. Make a copy of each group's completed skit, directing the group to highlight the errors on the copy for your reference.

As a group presents its skit, challenge each student in the audience to listen carefully and to make a list of any errors he catches. As students share their lists, have the performing group identify correct guesses. Not only will students learn more about your state's history, but they'll also add some shine to their listening skills!

Operation Alliteration

Skill: Reviewing important people and events in your state's history

Review important facts about your state's history with this letter-perfect project. Begin by having each student list interesting facts about your state's history. Next, have the student use a dictionary to list words that begin with the same letter as your state. As the final step, have the student use both lists—the state history facts and the word list—to write an alliterative paragraph about your state's history. For a fun display idea, have students cut out from old magazines samples of the letter they used. Then have each child glue some of the letters around the edges of a sheet of construction paper. Finally, have the student copy or glue her paragraph inside the frame of letters. Display the projects on a bulletin board titled "Presenting Pertinent Paragraphs About Our State's Past."

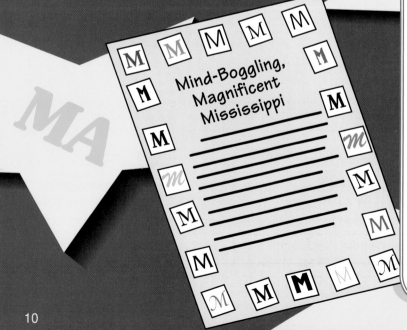

State History Time Capsule

Will you do a favor for the head honcho in your state? The governor has decided to put together a time capsule for the citizens of a future century. You have been selected to choose appropriate artifacts to represent the history of your state. Follow the steps given to help out your governor.

Steps:

1. In the box, list at least seven important events in your state's history.
2. Think about how each event impacted the people of your state and the nation. Then underline the five events that you think are the most important.
3. For each underlined event, draw a picture in the time capsule of an artifact that represents the event.
4. On a sheet of notebook paper, write a letter to the governor describing the artifacts you have chosen. Tell why you have selected each event featured in this time capsule.
5. Staple your letter to the back of this page.

★ Important State History Events ★

_____
_____
_____
_____
_____
_____
_____
_____
_____
_____
_____
_____

★   ★

Bonus Box: Number the five items in your time capsule from 1 to 5, with 1 being the most important event. On the back of this page, write a few sentences explaining why your number one item deserves that ranking.

Penny Patterns

Use with "A Penny for Your Thoughts" on page 10.

©The Mailbox® • *Social Studies* • TEC60939

Where Would We Be Without You?

Thomas Edison, Martin Luther King Jr., Eleanor Roosevelt—where would our country be without the contributions of these ingenious and gifted Americans? In the same way, your state has been home to many talented people who have made great contributions to your state and our country.

Directions: Choose a famous person from your state. Write the person's name where indicated. Then research to find out how this person has impacted your state. In strip 1, draw a cartoon that illustrates how life in your state is different because of this person's contributions. In strip 2, draw a cartoon that illustrates how life in your state would be different if this person had never been born.

Famous person in my state: _____

★ ★ ★ ★ ★ ★ ★ ★ ★ ★ ★ Strip 1 ★ ★ ★ ★ ★ ★ ★ ★ ★ ★ ★

★ ★ ★ ★ ★ ★ ★ ★ ★ ★ ★ Strip 2 ★ ★ ★ ★ ★ ★ ★ ★ ★ ★ ★

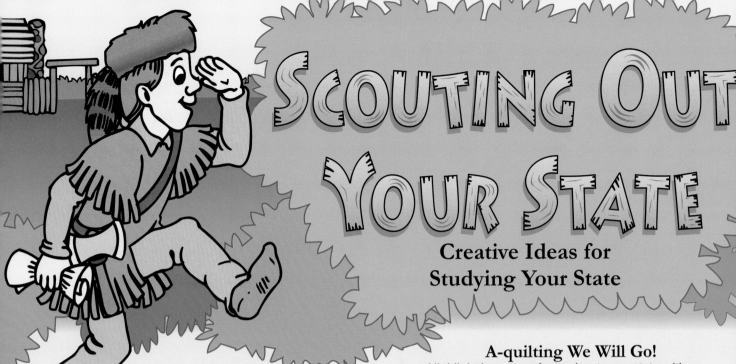

SCOUTING OUT YOUR STATE

Creative Ideas for Studying Your State

Looking to explore a new frontier while studying your state? Then scout out these exciting ideas and reproducibles that reveal your home state to students like never before!

with ideas by Michael Foster, Seneca, KS

Towering Totems

Honor your state's most famous citizens with an activity students will think is really fun! Collect a large clean coffee can for each student. Next, assign each student a different famous citizen to research. Then help the student divide a 6¾" x 20" strip of white bulletin board paper into thirds. Direct him to illustrate and label the three sections as follows:

- **First section:** a picture that illustrates an important event in that person's life
- **Center section:** a head-and-shoulders picture of the person, including his/her name
- **Third section:** a picture that shows what the person did to become famous

When the student has finished his drawings, have him wrap the strip around a can and tape it securely. Then have students sort the cans by category, such as history, government, the arts, etc. Stack each category's cans atop one another so that the center-section drawings are aligned. Then help students tape the cans together with transparent box-sealing tape to prevent toppling. What a towering way to honor the outstanding people of your outstanding state!

A-quilting We Will Go!

Highlight important facts about your state with an activity that will leave students in stitches! Give each student a copy of page 17 and the following materials: scissors, colorful construction paper scraps, a pencil, crayons, glue, and an eight-inch square of black construction paper. Then have her follow the directions on the page to create a quilt square. Mount the completed squares on a large sheet of bulletin board paper, alternating them with eight-inch squares of colorful construction paper. Showcase the resulting class quilt by hanging it on a wall with the title "Stitchin' Our State!"

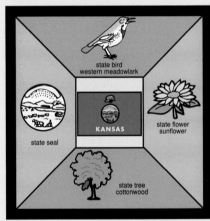

Manufacturing Mall

Show off your state's products with this idea that results in a mall students can call their own! After studying about the products your state manufactures, have each student (or pair of students) use various art materials and recyclables to create a large-scale model of one product. Next, have the student research information about that product, such as where it is manufactured, what raw materials are needed to make it, and how much money it brings into the state. Have the student make a chart that displays her data. Then set up the models and charts in your school's media center or an unused classroom to create a Manufacturing Mall. Invite other classes to visit the mall and learn about your state's products as students share their displays.

Singin' a New State Song

Review noteworthy facts about your home, sweet home with this stately song-writing activity. First, review with students important information about your state, such as its symbols, landforms, agriculture, products, etc. Next, have each student use what he's learned to write the lines (verse and chorus) of a new state song that can be sung to the melody of a familiar tune. After the student has written his lyrics, allow him to audition his song for the class. Have the class members vote on the best lyrics. Then duplicate the winning words so the whole class can sing along!

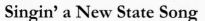

Native American Murals

Investigate the culture of your state's Native Americans with this art activity. Divide your class into small groups. Have each group research a different Native American culture of your state. Then have each group create a mural that depicts its assigned culture, using as many of the materials native to that culture as possible. For example, if the homes of one group's culture were made of sticks and grass, have the students who are researching that group use those materials when illustrating their mural. After the murals have been shared, display them in your school's hallways.

Great Gals Gallery

Introduce students to the great gals of your state's history with this research and art activity! Have each student research a different famous woman and then write an informative paragraph about her on a 3" x 5" index card. Next, have the student use the materials and the directions below to fashion a model of this lady. Arrange the completed models in your school's media center under a banner titled "[your state]'s Hall of Fame for Women" so that other classes can learn more about your state's great gals.

Materials for each student:
clean dish detergent bottle
2¹/₂-inch foam ball
hot glue gun (for teacher use only)
glue
2 wiggle eyes
scissors
stapler
2 craft sticks
markers
various art materials, such as yarn, fabric scraps, tissue and construction paper, buttons, etc.

Directions:
1. Have your teacher hot-glue the foam ball to the top of your bottle's cap.
2. With your teacher's help, make a vertical cut approximately ¹/₄-inch long on each side of your bottle near the top. Push a craft stick (arm) into each opening.
3. Glue the wiggle eyes to the ball. Use markers to add a nose and mouth. Use various materials to make hair, clothing, hands, and shoes. Then glue them to your bottle.
4. Staple your card to the model's hand or clothing.

15

You Were There!

Review your state's history by giving students some firsthand experience at hot-off-the-press news reporting. First, review with students the components of a good newspaper article: *who, what, when, where, why,* and *how.* Explain that many news articles also include quotations from eyewitnesses. Next, assign each student a different event related to your state's history. Have the student pretend that she was present when that event occurred. Then give her a copy of page 18 to complete as directed. Compile the finished front pages to create a special edition for your class library.

City Skyline Brochures

Send each student on a tour of one of your state's major cities with this one-of-a-kind research project. Assign each student a different city to research. Then give him a 12" x 18" sheet of construction paper, scissors, and crayons or markers. Direct the student to fold his paper into thirds and then to cut out a skyline shape along its top edge as shown. Next, have him follow these guidelines to design a brochure about his assigned city:

Front panel: name of city, population, map of state showing city's location
Three inside panels: history of city, year founded, attractions
Two back panels: landforms, climate
Encourage students to add illustrations to all of the panels, reminding them that the job of the brochure is to sell the reader on the city. When the brochures have been completed, provide time for students to share their projects. For another unbeatable brochure project, see the next idea.

adapted from an idea by Christie Hansen
Longs Creek Elementary
San Antonio, TX

A Great Place to Visit!

Get ready to introduce your state to *next* year's students with this nifty idea! Toward the end of the school year, have each student make a travel brochure about your state, including facts and information she learned this year. Collect these brochures. During the first week of the next school year, distribute the brochures to your new students to acquaint them with the sensational state they'll be studying.

Connie Fuller, Clay Elementary, Clay, AL

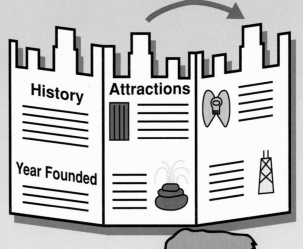

A-quilting We Will Go!

Quilting provided a way for pioneer women to remember important events and people. Follow the directions below to create a quilt square that will remind you of important facts about your state.

Directions:
1. Choose one of the following themes for your square: state symbols, historical events, famous people, products, climate, landforms.
2. Cut apart the five pieces of the pattern below. Then trace each piece on colorful paper and cut it out.
3. On each piece of paper, draw and label a different picture to illustrate the theme you selected. Then color your drawings.
4. Arrange the pieces back into a square on top of the black paper, leaving a margin all around (see the illustration). Glue the pieces in place.
5. Give your completed square to your teacher to help make a class quilt about your state.

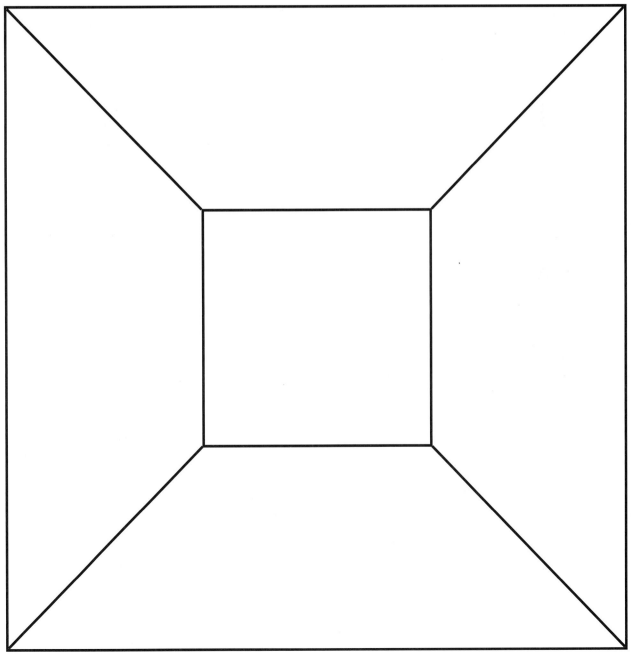

You Were There!

Pretend that you are a newspaper reporter and have just witnessed an important event in your state's history. Now you're going to be the first to print the story! Fill in the lines below to report the *who, what, when, where, why,* and *how* of the event you witnessed. Include a quotation from another eyewitness. Then write a second article about how people reacted to this event. Add pictures and fill in the blanks where indicated.

What's Inside
- Local News
- Business News
- _____ News
- _____ News
- _____ News

The _____ Centurion
(name of your state)

_____
(date)

STATE HISTORY MADE TODAY!

by _____
(your name)

_____
_____
_____
_____
_____
_____
_____
_____
_____
_____

(picture of historic event)

_____
_____

_____
(headline for article about how people reacted to this historic event)

_____
_____
_____
_____
_____
_____

(chart, graph, or map about historic event)

U.S. History

Colonial Kids
Growing Up in Colonial America

No televisions. No computers. Not even indoor plumbing. Life for the young people of colonial America was quite different from what today's children experience. Examine America's colonial period through the eyes of the kids who lived it using the following high-interest activities.

with contributions by Jennifer Roy, Saratoga Springs, NY

How Would You Feel?

Skills: Expressive writing, activating prior knowledge

How would you feel if you weren't able to bathe or shower for two whole months? Use attention-grabbing questions like this one, found on page 23, to generate interest in your colonial America unit. Just follow these steps:

1. Make one or two copies of the question cards on page 23 (so that you have a card for each student).
2. Cut out the cards and place them in a paper bag.
3. Have each student draw a card from the bag and read it silently. Then have him write an answer to the question in his journal.
4. Ask each child to read his question and answer aloud. Invite other students to add their thoughts.

If desired, end the activity by posting a chart like the one shown. With students, fill in the first three columns. Have students complete the last section of the chart as they learn more about colonial America.

Colonial America			
What we already know	What we want to learn	How we'll locate information to answer the questions	What we've learned

Preparing the paper:
Brew a cup of tea. Let the bag steep for five to ten minutes; then let the tea cool and remove the bag. Gently squeeze the tea bag and dab it on your paper. Let the paper dry completely. If desired, gently tear the edges to give the paper a weathered look.

Colonial Names
Humility
Remember
Resolved
Desire
Love
Patience
Charity
Constant
Unity
Experience
Waitstill
Preserved
Thanks
Unite
Supply

What's in a Name?

Skills: Vocabulary, implied meanings, expressive writing

What's in a name? Plenty if you lived in colonial times. Colonial children were sometimes named for traits that the parents thought were important. That's why a roll call of children who were on the *Mayflower* includes such names as Resolved, Humility, and Desire.

After sharing the information about the naming of colonial children, challenge students to play the name game themselves! First, brainstorm with students a list of the difficulties colonists faced, such as lack of farming skills, harsh winters, sickness, etc. Next, display the list of colonial children's names shown and divide the class into groups of two or three students each. Have each group choose a name from the list and research its meaning using a dictionary. Then have the group write a diary entry from one of the child's parents explaining why that name was chosen and how the child might need to demonstrate the trait as a new settler. When the entries are finished, have each group use a black pen to copy its work onto a sheet of white paper. Then demonstrate for each group how to transform its paper into an authentic-looking document using the directions shown. Post the papers on a bulletin board labeled "My Name Is…"

Attention, Colonial Mart Shoppers!

Skill: Researching a topic

In the early days of colonial America, there were no stores for colonists who wanted to shop till they dropped. But what if there had been? Invite your students to open the first ever Colonial Mart superstore with an activity that explores the daily life of colonial America. First, show students examples of ad circulars and catalogs from large stores like Wal-Mart or Target. Point out that the ads are often organized according to different departments, such as children's clothing, electronics, and toys. Let students examine the ad pieces in small groups.

Next, divide the class into the store departments shown. Provide each group with two sheets of art paper, crayons or markers, and reference materials about daily life in colonial America. Then instruct each group to create two (or more) pages for a catalog advertising the first superstore in colonial America, Colonial Mart. On its pages, have each group illustrate several colonial American items that might be sold in its department, including each item's name, price, and a description of how a colonist used it. Combine the group's pages between two covers to create your colonial catalog. For a variation that practices oral-presentation skills, challenge students to create commercials instead of catalog pages.

Clothing

GROCERY
(food and drink)

Housewares
(household tools)

Hardware
(tools for farms
and trades)

Home Furnishings

Toys and Games

Pharmacy
(medicines and
health care items)

Women's Wear
Colonial Mart

Calash
Protect your do from disaster!
Originally $1.99
Sale $0.99

Dress
With fitted bodice
and lovely stomacher
(Petticoat and
pocket-hoop
farthingale not
included.)
$12.99

Pocket-Hoop
Farthingale
Make your
waist look as
thin as a rod!
$2.99

Clogs
Protect your prettiest shoes!
$0.99 per pair

Home of the Free?

Skills: Critical thinking, making connections

Not all people who lived in colonial America would have called it the home of the free. African Americans and Native Americans were both adversely affected by colonization. Slaves knew oppression, while Native Americans saw their land being taken over by the growing population of colonists. Discuss these two groups with students. Then ask, "If you were a young slave or Native American in colonial America, what traits would you need to survive?" After students reflect on this question, divide the class into six teams. Provide each team with a large sheet of chart paper, three copies of the wheel pattern on page 24, and a marker. Direct three teams to label the tops of their papers "African Americans" and three to label their papers "Native Americans." Then guide the teams through these steps:

1. Brainstorm a list of personality traits that children in your group would need to survive in colonial America. List these words across the top of your paper.
2. Cut out the wheel patterns.
3. Choose three traits from the list and write each one in the center of a different wheel.
4. In the spaces between the spokes of each wheel, write five ways that kids today can demonstrate that trait. Glue the wheels below the word list.

When the charts are finished, pair each African American team with a Native American team. Then have teams share their charts, comparing and contrasting the difficulties faced by each group.

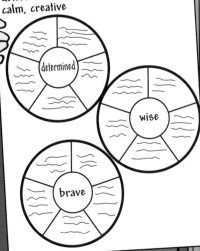
Native Americans
determined, brave, patient, wise, enduring, calm, creative

determined

wise

brave

Easy As A, B, C

Skills: Poetry, alliteration, penmanship

One of the items that helped the colonial child learn his letters and numbers was a folded card called a *battledore.* Battledores, which cost parents only a penny each, were printed with the alphabet, numbers, small pictures, and rhymes.

Use the reproducible activity on page 25 to help students make their own colonial battledores. Provide each child with a copy of page 25, scissors, and crayons or markers. Have the student complete the page as directed. Then discuss with students how learning to read and write with a battledore was different from how children learn in today's schools.

A Little Time for Fun

Skills: Mental math, addition

Life for colonial children may have been mostly work, but there was time to play. Smart colonial parents sneaked in a little math education using two games: ninepin and five alleys. Play your own versions of these fun games following the directions below.

- **Ninepin:** Collect nine empty Pringles potato chip cans and one small ball. Display a copy of the rules shown. Ask students if they recognize a pattern in the scoring rules (each successive goal after 39 is nine pins larger than the one before it). Then have students follow these rules:
  1. Set up the cans in three rows of three or one long row of nine.
  2. In turn, each player rolls the ball to knock over the pins. The player scores one point for each pin knocked down. He resets the pins after each roll.
  3. The first player to score 31 points (with no leftover pins) is the winner.
  4. If a player knocks down more than 31 pins, he must then try to get a score of 39.
  5. If a player knocks down more than 39 pins, he must next try for a score of 48 (then 57, 66, and so on).
  6. The first player to reach one of the goal numbers is the winner.

- **Five Alleys:** The Pilgrims made a wooden box that was divided into five alleys at one end, each labeled with a number. A child rolled a small ball from one end of the box into one of the alleys at the other end and added the number rolled to his running total. The player with the higher score at the end of ten rolls was the winner. To make the game, tape five small paper cups to one end of the bottom or lid of a large gift box; then write a different two- or three-digit number on each cup as shown. Slightly elevate the end of the box without the cups. Each player, in turn, rolls a marble or small ball from the elevated end of the box into one of the cups; then he writes that number on his paper. On his next turn, the player adds the number he rolls to the first number. The winner is the player with the higher score after ten rolls.

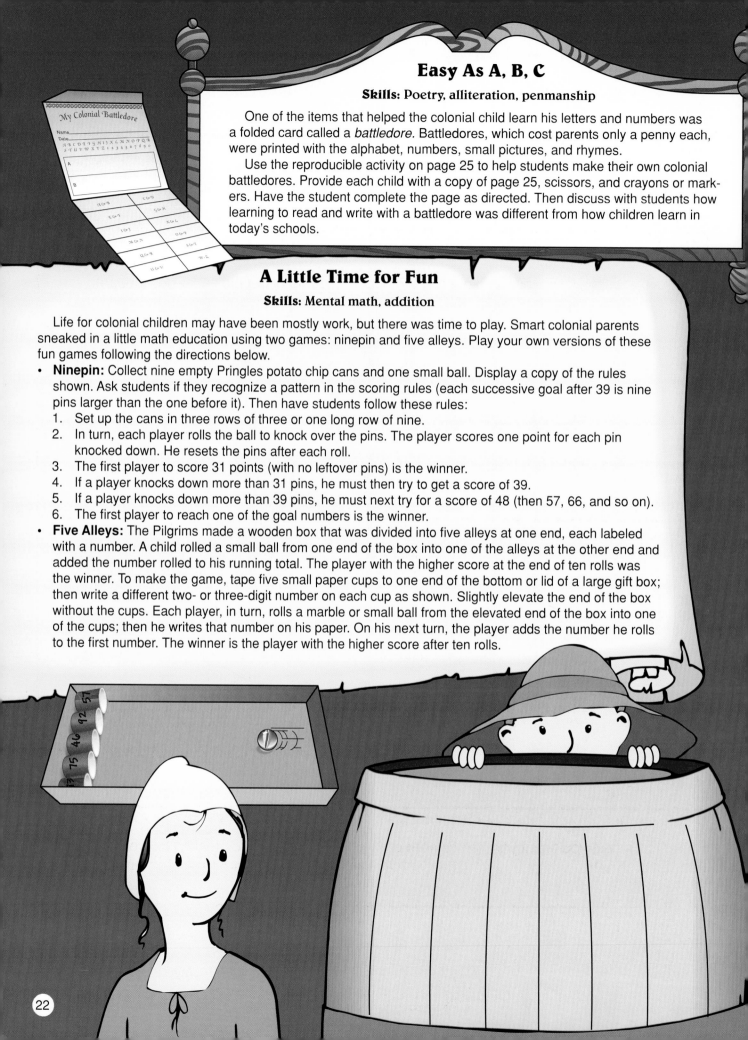

1. How would you feel if you had to say good-bye to all of your family and friends, knowing you'd never see them again?

2. How would you feel about working for someone for five to seven years without being paid?

3. How would you feel if you weren't able to bathe or shower for two whole months?

4. How would you feel if a strange-looking group of people suddenly appeared in your yard?

5. How would you feel if your house were blown down during a storm?

6. How would you feel about living with your entire family in a one-room house?

7. How would you feel if you weren't allowed to sit during meals?

8. How would you feel if your father announced that your family had just run out of food?

9. How would you feel if you only owned two or three outfits to wear?

10. How would you feel if you rarely saw your parents or any other grown-ups during the day?

11. How would you feel about being in a family with 12 brothers and sisters?

12. How would you feel if your mom and dad were your teachers?

13. How would you feel if you spent more time doing chores than you did being with friends, going to school, or playing?

14. How would you feel about never brushing your teeth?

15. How would you feel if you had to work on Christmas?

16. How would you feel if you were not allowed to learn to read or write?

Wheel Pattern

Use with "Home of the Free?" on page 21.

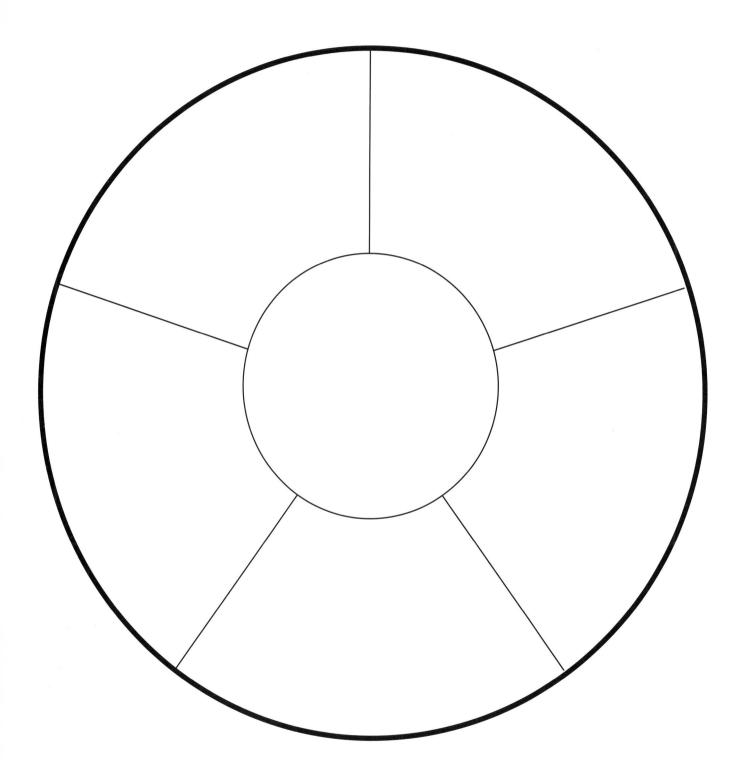

My Colonial Battledore

My Colonial Battledore

Name _____

Date _____

*A B C D E F G H I J K L M N O P Q R
S T U V W X Y Z 1 2 3 4 5 6 7 8 9 0*

A	
B	

A & B	*C & D*
E & F	*G & H*
I & J	*K & L*
M & N	*O & P*
Q & R	*S & T*
U & V	*W–Z*

Some colonial children learned to read and write using a small folded card called a *battledore*. A battledore included letters, numbers, small pictures, and rhymes. Use your best handwriting to make your own battledore. Follow these steps:

1. In box A, write a two-line rhyming verse that states a rule for everyday living.
   Example:
   Always listening, always kind,
   A better friend you'll never find.
2. Choose a letter of the alphabet. In box B, write an alliterative sentence made mostly of words that begin with that letter.
   Example:
   Betsy bought a blue blouse and a brown belt.
3. In each letter box, write a vocabulary word you would like to learn that begins with one of the box's letters. Look for words in the books you're reading, your textbooks, or the dictionary.
4. Cut out the battledore and fold it on the dotted lines.
5. Decorate the front of the folded battledore.

Note to the teacher: Use with "Easy As A, B, C" on page 22.

25

America's Industrial

Between 1850 and 1900, America began to grow as never before. The results of the growth spurt—both positive and negative—changed our country forever. Introduce your students to this important chapter in our nation's history with the following creative activities.

with ideas by Wanda Helmuth, Fort Collins, CO

Movin' to the City

Concept: The growth of cities during the Industrial Revolution

The Industrial Revolution was a time of great change. Help students keep track of those changes with the help of a stunning display. Cover a bulletin board with white paper; then divide it in half as shown. Have one group of students color half of the board with red, orange, and yellow chalk, smudging the colors to create a sunriselike effect. Ask another group to color the other half with blue, pink, and purple chalk. Have a third group attach farm silhouettes (barn, tree, silo, etc.) cut from black paper to the board as shown. Direct a fourth group to add a city skyline cut from black paper and the title "My, How Things Changed!"

Explain to students that one change during the Industrial Revolution was that America's economy began to move away from farming and toward industry, as illustrated by the country/city display. During the unit, challenge each student to write on a paper cloud cutout one other way that America changed during the Industrial Revolution (see the background information at the left). Then have him pin the cloud to the display. Review the clouds periodically throughout the unit.

Industrial Revolution Fast Facts

Industry in the United States grew after the Civil War because

- there were lots of raw materials
- the United States population grew, which meant more consumers and more workers
- the railroad industry, which could transport raw materials and goods, grew rapidly
- new inventions and machines made production cheaper and quicker
- there were few government restrictions on business

Because of the Industrial Revolution

- more jobs and opportunities were created
- people moved to cities in huge numbers
- millions of immigrants flocked to America for the jobs and a better life
- more machinery was used to produce goods, leading to a greater division of labor
- only a few people got wealthy, while many others faced extreme poverty
- living and working conditions in cities were often dangerous and unhealthy

My, How Things Changed!

Revolution

Coming to America

Concept: Immigration during the Industrial Revolution

About 28 million immigrants flocked to America between 1830 and 1910. Those who arrived from 1870 on moved to cities and created a new workforce for industry. Explore this movement of people—the largest ever—with the following research and creative-dramatics activity. With your media specialist's help, share books about immigration with students. Then divide the class into groups. Give each group a copy of the following research questions:

- Why did immigrants want to come to America during this time period?
- What was the trip to America like for the average immigrant?
- What was Ellis Island, and why was it important to immigrants? What happened to an immigrant at Ellis Island?
- What challenges did new immigrants face in America? How was life different for them?

After students research the questions, have each team use what it has learned to write a news program titled "Live From Ellis Island." Direct each team to choose one student to be a news anchor interviewing immigrants and others at Ellis Island (such as medical personnel, security guards, relatives, businesspeople looking for laborers, etc.). Videotape the programs or have students present them live for other classes.

Caution: Kids at Work

Concept: Child labor during the Industrial Revolution

During the Industrial Revolution, children often worked as unskilled laborers in the growing number of factories. Many worked ten to 14 hours a day, six days a week, in dangerous or unhealthy conditions. Get students thinking about this not-so-pretty aspect of the Industrial Revolution with the reproducible on page 30. After each student completes the page as directed, have her create a brochure to persuade the public that her new child labor laws should be adopted.

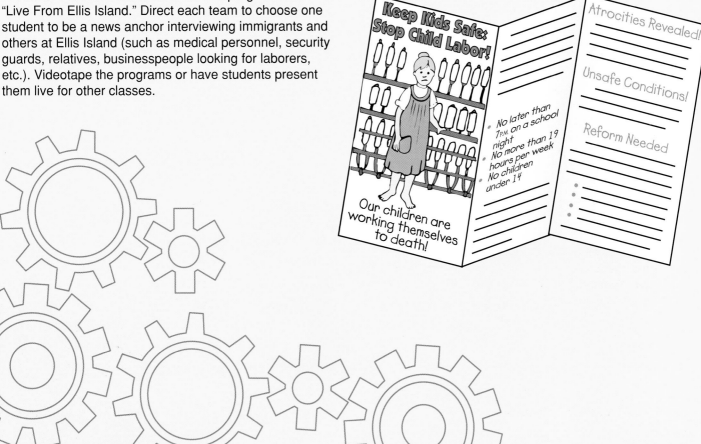

We're on a Roll!

During the Industrial Revolution, workers began to work on assembly lines, mass-producing products. Give students a glimpse of what it might have been like to work on an assembly line by making a batch of itty-bitty burgers!

Preparing for the activity:

1. Write each station's task (see below) on a separate index card.
2. Position five student desks in a row at the front of the room. Tape a labeled index card on each desktop.
3. Place the following materials on each desk.*

    Station 1: vanilla wafer cookies (2 per student); small paper plates (2 per student)
    Station 2: tube of yellow decorator frosting
    Station 3: 1/2 cup flaked coconut, tinted green; plastic spoon
    Station 4: thin chocolate mint cookies (2 per student)
    Station 5: tube of red decorator frosting; vanilla wafer cookies (2 per student)

Be sure to have a few extras of each material on hand for demonstrations.

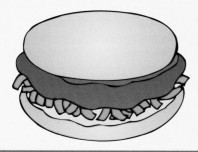

Doing the activity:

Remind students that the goal of the assembly line is to produce quality products in a short amount of time. Explain that before machinery, products were made by hand by one worker. Demonstrate by making one burger as the class times you. Write this time on the board. Then have students predict how long it will take five students on an assembly line to make one burger. After writing this prediction on the board, choose five volunteers to man the stations. Time the students as they make one burger, assembly-line fashion, using the steps in the box. Write the time on the board beside the prediction. Then restart the timer and have the assembly line make nine more. Write the time used on the board. Then call up five different volunteers and time them as they complete ten burgers. Repeat until each student has participated in the assembly line.

While students munch on their completed cookie burgers, discuss the positive effects of this production method *(can make more products more quickly and at a lower cost, doesn't require highly skilled workers, workers can learn a job quickly, some work could be done by robots today, etc.).* Then talk about the negative effects *(can get boring doing same task over and over, worker doesn't learn a real skill and so doesn't get paid very high wages, boredom can result in carelessness, etc.).*

Itty-Bitty Burger Assembly Line Stations

Station 1: Put one vanilla wafer upside down on a paper plate.
Station 2: Squeeze yellow frosting on a vanilla wafer (mustard, bottom of bun).
Station 3: Top mustard with green-tinted coconut (lettuce).
Station 4: Top lettuce with thin mint cookie (burger).
Station 5: Squeeze red frosting on another vanilla wafer (ketchup, top of bun); add to top of hamburger.

Noteworthy Newsmakers

Introduce students to the newsmakers who played important roles in the Industrial Revolution with the following research activity. Divide the class into pairs. Ask each twosome to choose ten people from the list shown. Then give the pair ten copies of the trading card below. Have the students research their famous folks and complete a card for each according to the directions. Finally, have the pair create a ten-question quiz about its people, storing it with the cards and an answer key in a large zippered plastic bag.

After collecting the bags, redistribute them to the student pairs. Have each duo read the cards in its bag, complete the quiz, and check with the key. Rotate the bags among student pairs until each twosome has read at least three different sets of cards. Then collect the bags and place them in your class library for more free-time browsing.

Name: ___
Cardmak___

Name: *Lillian D. Wald*
Cardmakers: *Meredith and Stacey*

Inventors: Alexander Graham Bell, Thomas Edison, Henry Ford, Jan Matzeliger, Elijah McCoy, George Westinghouse, Christopher L. Sholes, Emile Berliner, George Eastman, Elias Howe
Businesspeople: Philip D. Armour, Andrew Carnegie, Andrew W. Mellon, John D. Rockefeller, Cornelius Vanderbilt, Gustavus Swift, Charles A. Pillsbury, James B. Duke, Frank W. Woolworth
Labor Leaders and Social Activists: Eugene V. Debs, Uriah S. Stephens, Samuel Gompers, Mary Harris "Mother" Jones, Jane Addams, Lillian D. Wald, Julia C. Lathrop, Florence Kelley

Trading Card Pattern
Use with "Noteworthy Newsmakers" above.

Directions:
1. Fill in both boxes with a fine-tip marker or pen. In the left box, illustrate the person or one of his/her accomplishments.
2. Color the boxes lightly.
3. Cut along the bold lines.
4. Fold along the dotted line. Then glue the two boxes together to make one trading card.

Draw a picture here.

Name: _____

Cardmakers: _____

Born: _____

Died: _____

Major accomplishment during the Industrial Revolution: _____

_____

_____

_____

How this accomplishment changed America:

_____

_____

_____

_____

Caution: Kids at Work

Part 1: Read the following article. Highlight or underline key points.

Have you ever wished that you could get a job instead of going to school? That actually happened to many children during the Industrial Revolution. Children often worked in America's growing number of factories. They were hired to do jobs that didn't require them to know a skill. Children ran sewing machines and other pieces of machinery. They painted tins of canned meat and sorted feathers for hats. Some kids fed heavy, wet clothes into huge ironing machines or helped make products like cigar boxes and gloves. Many of these kids weren't even ten years old when they were hired. They worked from ten to 14 hours a day for six days a week. And because they were children, they earned very little money for their work.

There were other disadvantages for these working kids. Some children were badly injured or crippled by the unsafe machines. Many got sick from the unhealthy conditions in the factories. Most were very poor and couldn't read or write. Because they worked, these children couldn't attend school. But since many came from poor families, they continued to want these jobs. By 1890, almost one out of every five children in America worked in a factory.

People began to realize that something needed to be done to protect these children. They worked to get laws passed that restricted the hiring of children. Today, all 50 states have child labor laws that limit the employment of children.

Part 2: Pretend that you have visited factories and seen children working during the Industrial Revolution. Now you want to help write laws that will protect these kids. Fill out the chart below with information to include in your laws. Use the back if you need more space.

	Reason
Minimum age for being hired: _____	
Maximum number of hours allowed to work each day: ____ Maximum number of hours allowed to work each week: ____	
Prohibitions about working night hours:	
Types of work that children should not be hired to do:	
Other regulations:	

Part 3: On the back of this page or another sheet of paper, write five child labor laws that were needed during the Industrial Revolution. Use the information in your chart.

Name _____

Because...

The Industrial Revolution was a time when American industry grew and grew. There were several reasons, or *causes*, for this growth. On the factory's lines, list as many different causes for this growth as you can.

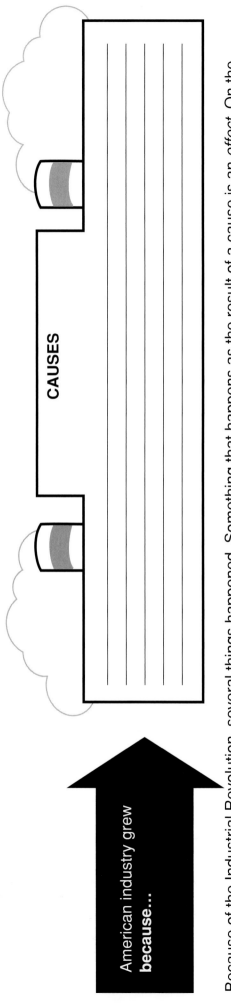

CAUSES

American industry grew **because...**

Because of the Industrial Revolution, several things happened. Something that happens as the result of a cause is an *effect*. On the factory's lines, list as many different effects of the Industrial Revolution as you can.

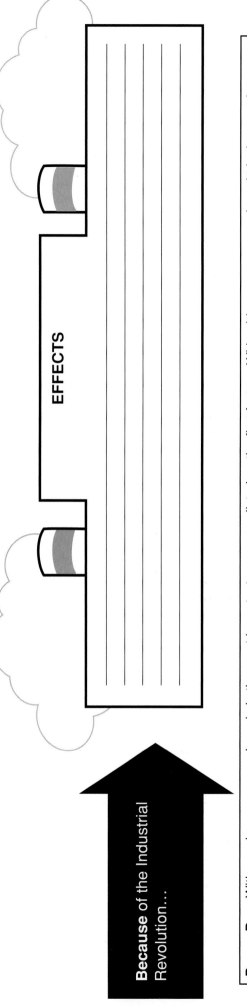

EFFECTS

Because of the Industrial Revolution...

Bonus Box: With a red crayon or marker, circle the most important cause you listed on the first factory. With a blue crayon or marker, circle the most important effect on the second factory. On the back of this page or another sheet of paper, write one or more sentences explaining your choices.

Voyage to the Colonies

All aboard for the American colonies! Set sail with this easy-to-do simulation that whips writing, research, math, and critical-thinking skills into shipshape condition!

from an idea by Kristina Sipe, Santa Sophia Academy, Spring Valley, CA

1 Preparing to Weigh Anchor

Launch this project by gathering reference materials and books about the first colonists. Make two copies of the cards on page 34. Cut the cards apart and put them in a bag. Also duplicate page 33 for each student.

Begin by discussing your students' thoughts and questions about what life was like in the Old World in the 1700s. Why do students think some people wanted to move to the New World? Would life be better there? How? What things would be needed on such a long journey? How did colonists probably feel about making such an important decision? Next, invite each student to become a passenger on a ship that's heading to the New World, *The [your school's name]*. Have each student draw a card from the bag to determine his identity on this exciting voyage. Point out that the cards list males (except the "stowaway" card) because during that time period the man tended to be the family member with a trade or occupation.

2 Setting Sail

Head out to sea by giving each student a copy of page 33, which lists the steps in this project. Discuss the sheet together and how it is organized by legs. After pointing out the location of the reference materials, have students start working on the first leg of their trip.

3 On the Open Seas

Sail on as students continue working on the assignments listed on page 33. As ship captain, periodically announce an unusual experience for students to include in their stories (for example, a storm throwing the ship off course or an unscheduled stop at a Caribbean island). Also suggest that students have different passengers (classmates) interact in their stories (for example, one passenger buying or trading goods with another). As stories are completed, put them in a three-ring binder. Read a different completed story at the beginning of each day's social studies lesson.

4 Arriving in the Colonies

Before students make land (Leg 4), spend time reviewing the colonies' different geographic regions. Also design a manifest page for the binder that lists each passenger's name and occupation, with room for each passenger's signature. Have students organize their stories in the binder according to the manifest. Then place the book in your school's media center for others to enjoy.

5 Side Excursions

Extend this project by sending students on the following side trips:

- Chart the ship's course from the Old World to the colonies on a map.
- Set up a log of itemized travel expenses.
- Survey the passengers to determine the geographic regions in which they settled. Graph the results.
- Evaluate each passenger's occupation in terms of how important it is to the success of his colony.

Comin' to America

Why would someone want to come to America from his or her homeland? What would it have been like to travel for many months on a ship across the ocean? What things would people need to take with them on such a journey? Answer these questions and more as you pretend to be a passenger on a ship headed to America!

Directions:

1. Pretend you are the passenger described on your card. Give this person and each of his family members a name.
2. Write a story to tell about each leg of the trip. You can write your stories in the form of a personal narrative, a journal entry, a letter, a mystery, or a humorous tale.
3. Use reference materials and other books to add facts to your stories to make them more believable.
4. Edit your stories; then write your final copies as neatly as you can.
5. As you complete each story, color its trunk. Give the story to your teacher to put into a class book.
6. When you have completed all your stories, sign your name on the ship's manifest (the table of contents) in the class book.

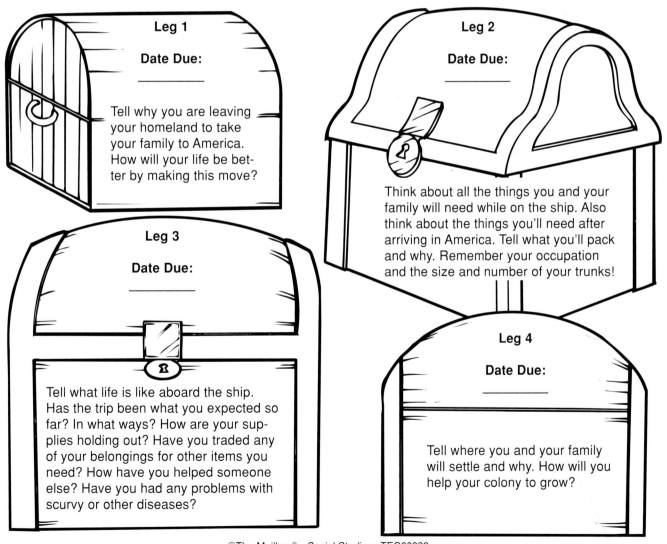

Leg 1

Date Due:

_____

Tell why you are leaving your homeland to take your family to America. How will your life be better by making this move?

Leg 2

Date Due:

_____

Think about all the things you and your family will need while on the ship. Also think about the things you'll need after arriving in America. Tell what you'll pack and why. Remember your occupation and the size and number of your trunks!

Leg 3

Date Due:

_____

Tell what life is like aboard the ship. Has the trip been what you expected so far? In what ways? How are your supplies holding out? Have you traded any of your belongings for other items you need? How have you helped someone else? Have you had any problems with scurvy or other diseases?

Leg 4

Date Due:

_____

Tell where you and your family will settle and why. How will you help your colony to grow?

©The Mailbox® • *Social Studies* • TEC60939

Note to the teacher: Use with the activities on page 32 and the cards on page 34. Before duplicating, fill in the due date for each assignment.

33

Passenger Cards

Use with "Preparing to Weigh Anchor" on page 32 and "Comin' to America" on page 33.

Passenger: cobbler
Family: wife, 2 children
Money: $350
Baggage: 1 trunk

Passenger: silversmith
Family: wife, 5 children
Money: $500
Baggage: 2 trunks

Passenger: nobleman
Family: wife, 2 children
Money: $1,000
Baggage: 4 trunks

Passenger: stowaway
Family: none
Money: $50
Baggage: knapsack

Passenger: candlemaker
Family: wife, 4 children
Money: $400
Baggage: 2 trunks

Passenger: farmer
Family: wife, 5 children
Money: $400
Baggage: 2 chickens, 1 cow, 2 trunks

Passenger: blacksmith
Family: wife, 3 children
Money: $500
Baggage: 2 trunks

Passenger: cooper
Family: wife, 2 children
Money: $450
Baggage: 1 trunk

Passenger: clockmaker
Family: wife, 3 children
Money: $500
Baggage: 2 trunks

Passenger: wheelwright
Family: wife, 4 children
Money: $500
Baggage: 2 trunks

Passenger: miller
Family: wife, 2 children
Money: $400
Baggage: 1 trunk

Passenger: tailor
Family: wife, 3 children
Money: $500
Baggage: 2 trunks

She Makes History a Hit!

Using Jean Fritz's Books to Teach U.S. History

With diverse casts of characters and story lines, author Jean Fritz skillfully weaves fact and fiction together to paint a picture of the past that delights young readers. Use the following activities based on Fritz's popular history books to introduce your students to the people and events that have helped shape history.

by Simone Lepine

Suggested Fritz Titles to Use With These Activities

- *Can't You Make Them Behave, King George?*
- *Where Was Patrick Henry on the 29th of May?*
- *Why Don't You Get a Horse, Sam Adams?*
- *Shh! We're Writing the Constitution*
- *Just a Few Words, Mr. Lincoln: The Story of the Gettysburg Address*

- *And Then What Happened, Paul Revere?*
- *What's the Big Idea, Ben Franklin?*
- *Will You Sign Here, John Hancock?*
- *Who's That Stepping on Plymouth Rock?*

Activities to Use With Any of Fritz's Historical Titles

Reading Response Booklet

Use this easy-to-make booklet to custom-tailor your class's study of Jean Fritz's books. From the list on this page, choose the books that you want your students to read. Provide each student with a half sheet of paper for each book you selected and two half sheets of construction paper to use as booklet covers. Have the student stack the sheets and staple them between the construction paper covers to make a booklet; then have him decorate the cover. Provide each student with a copy of the reading response cards on page 37; then direct him to cut out the cards of the books the class will be reading. Next, have the student glue one card to the top of each right-hand page in his booklet. After the student reads one of the books, have him complete the activity page for it.

Fun With Jean Fritz's Books
Reading Response Booklet

Name **Roy**

Why Do You Title Books With Questions, Jean Fritz?

Explore Jean Fritz's unique approach to titling her books with this activity. Show your students a collection of Jean Fritz's work. Ask students to point out the book titles that are questions. Have each student act as if he were the historical figure to whom each question is addressed. Then have the student write the book title along with the answer he thinks the character would give. For example, a student might respond that Patrick Henry—the main character in *Where Was Patrick Henry on the 29th of May?*—would answer the question posed in his book's title by saying, "I was giving an emotional speech to my fellow countrymen!" Challenge your students to make up additional book titles based on historical events and people about which Jean Fritz has not written. Provide students with the example of a book about Harriet Tubman that could be titled *How Did You Find Your Way, Harriet Tubman?*

If I Knew Then What I Know Now!

Jean Fritz's books stand out in the sea of nonfiction because she has a knack for bringing well-known historical figures and events to life. Before reading one of Fritz's books, have each student make a two-column chart like the one shown. Instruct the student to record what she already knows about the individual or historical event from textbooks and other sources in the "Before Reading" column. Then have the student read Fritz's book that pertains to that subject or person. When the student finishes reading the story, have her list any new facts she has learned. Conclude by having the student explain how reading Fritz's story helped her better understand this topic or person.

| What I Know About John Hancock ||
Before Reading	After Reading
He was a patriot.	He was very wealthy and threw big parties.
He signed the Declaration of Independence.	He lived in a house with 54 windows.
He was from New England.	He signed the Declaration of Independence large so that King George, even without his glasses, was sure to see his signature.
He did not like the way England was treating the colonies.	He was disliked by King George because he refused to pay taxes.

T-Shirt Trivia

Looking for a fun way for your students to share what they've learned from reading Jean Fritz's biographies? Divide your class into groups. Assign each group a Fritz biography the class has read. Provide each group with a T-shirt cut from construction paper. Direct each group to write the name of the person upon whose life the biography was based in the center of the T-shirt. On a separate sheet of paper, have the group list the things it learned about the person from reading the story. Then have the group draw symbols and write words to represent each fact on its T-shirt. Invite each group to share its shirt with the rest of the class and explain what each picture or symbol represents. Display the completed T-shirts on a bulletin board titled "Jean Fritz's Biographies Are 'Tee-rrific'!"

Famous Resumés

Ask your students the following question: Which individual would you hire: Ben Franklin, King George, or Paul Revere? Explain that one way an employer decides whom to hire is by looking over each person's *resumé*—a personal summary of job experience and accomplishments. Show students samples from a book on how to write a resume. Point out the information that each resumé includes: *name, address, education, job experience,* and *achievements.* Next, divide your students into seven groups. Provide each group with one of Fritz's biographies. Have each group read its book together and keep a record of the jobs, experience, and accomplishments of the person upon whose life the story is based. Then instruct each group to use the information it gathers to write a resume for the individual.

Extend the activity by holding a job fair. Select several job advertisements from the newspaper's classified ads. Write the job titles on the board and have a member from each group copy them onto a sheet of paper. Read each job description aloud to your students. As you read each description, have each group write an explanation as to whether its famous person would be qualified for the job. Once you have read all the job descriptions aloud, have each group share its responses and explain its decisions.

Monuments-R-Us!

Your students will approach this "monumental" task with great enthusiasm! After reading several biographies by Jean Fritz, read aloud *Who's That Stepping on Plymouth Rock?,* the story of how Plymouth Rock became a national landmark. Ask the following questions: Why did the people of Plymouth want to make a monument out of the rock? Why do nations create monuments, and why do people visit them? What are some monuments you have visited or heard about? What can people learn from monuments? When the discussion is complete, have each student design a monument in honor of one of the individuals or historic events about which he has recently read. Explain that the monument's design should reflect the importance of the individual or event. Then have each student draw or construct a small-scale model of the monument. Provide time for each student to share his completed monument with the class and explain his design.

Why Don't You Get a Horse, Samuel Adams?

1. Draw a picture showing how Samuel Adams dressed at the beginning of the book; then write a description of his appearance.
2. Why do you think Samuel Adams would not ride a horse? Name one thing you dislike doing and explain why you dislike it.
3. Pretend you are Samuel Adams. Write a short speech outlining your opinions on England's role in the colonies and America's independence.

Will You Sign Here, John Hancock?

1. List and describe John Hancock's nine *conveyances*, or vehicles. Why do you suppose he had so many?
2. Explain why you think the Continental Congress chose George Washington over John Hancock as commander in chief of the army.
3. John Hancock was one of the richest men in the colonies. Find three details in the book that support that statement.

Shh! We're Writing the Constitution

1. Describe the government organization proposed in Edmund Randolph's Virginia Plan.
2. Why were some delegates opposed to organizing the government as proposed by Randolph?
3. Pretend you are a delegate at the convention. Write a letter home to your family describing the summer's events.

Who's That Stepping on Plymouth Rock?

1. Make a timeline that shows how Plymouth Rock got to its present location.
2. Do you think the first Pilgrims really stepped on Plymouth Rock? Explain your answer.
3. Name your favorite historical monument. Describe what the monument represents and why it is your favorite.

Just a Few Words, Mr. Lincoln: The Story of the Gettysburg Address

1. Pretend you are living during the time of the Civil War. Write a letter to President Lincoln describing your feelings about the war.
2. List what you think are the two most important points covered in President Lincoln's speech.
3. Choose five words you are not familiar with from President Lincoln's speech. Look up each word in the dictionary and write its meaning in your own words.

Fun With Jean Fritz's Books
Reading Response Booklet

©The Mailbox® • Social Studies • TEC60939

Name _____

Can't You Make Them Behave, King George?

1. Pretend you are King George. Explain why the colonists should pay taxes.
2. After reading pages 24–31, make up your own list of five rules that a good king should follow.
3. What do you think would have happened if the colonists had not won the war? Describe how things would have been different.

And Then What Happened, Paul Revere?

1. Make a list of Paul Revere's many jobs and skills.
2. Pretend you are Paul Revere. Write an entry in your journal describing the Boston Tea Party.
3. Make a map that shows the location of important events that occurred along the route of Paul Revere's famous ride.

Where Was Patrick Henry on the 29th of May?

1. What were some of the jobs Patrick Henry tried and was unsuccessful at before he found out he had a gift for speaking?
2. Write out the words to Patrick Henry's famous speech on pages 36 and 37. Then reenact the speech with the help of several classmates.
3. Write a short speech on an issue you feel strongly about. Then deliver the speech to your class.

What's the Big Idea, Ben Franklin?

1. After reading Ben Franklin's list of rules for good behavior (page 21), make up your own list of ten rules for good behavior.
2. List some of Ben Franklin's inventions that are described in the book. Then plan an invention of your own by drawing a diagram of it. Write a paragraph describing what the invention can do.
3. Write a poem about Ben Franklin's interesting life.

BACK TO THE PAST

Creative Ideas for Bringing History to Life

Need a fresh, new approach for teaching history? You don't have to travel far! Just check out the following collection of ideas from our readers!

TIME-TRAVELING TOURISTS

Invite your students to visit ancient Rome or the site of the Battle of Gettysburg by becoming travel agents! First, divide students into five or six travel agencies. Assign each agency a time-travel destination, such as a decade or an era that is part of your unit of study. Then direct each agency to write and illustrate a brochure that gives information on the following topics related to that time period:

- historical events
- celebrations
- customs
- places to visit
- styles of clothing
- types of transportation available
- travel advisories for problems such as the plague or hostile enemies
- climate/seasonal conditions

After the brochures are completed, have each group try to sell the rest of the class on the exciting travel possibilities of taking its trip. Encourage your travel agents to wear costumes, make tickets, and create travel posters to add an exciting twist to their time-traveling testimonies! *Terry Healy, Eugene Field Elementary, Manhattan, KS*

I forgot to study for my social studies test.

I didn't make a good grade on the test.

My mom and dad were pretty sore.

I was grounded for a whole week.

I couldn't go to Jody's sleepover.

ONE THING LEADS TO ANOTHER

Help students see that history is a series of cause-and-effect relationships with this unique hands-on activity. Provide each student with five construction paper strips. On his first strip, have the student write an event that has recently happened in his life. On his second strip, instruct the student to write the effect caused by the first event. Then, on his third strip, have the student write the effect caused by the second event, and so on until he completes five strips. Next, have the student use tape to link the strips together into a chain—a literal chain of events! When studying important historical events, use this hands-on idea to help students better understand how historical events are connected to each other. *Marie Altenburg, Lindenhurst Middle School, Lindenhurst, NY*

UP CLOSE AND PERSONAL

Who wouldn't jump at the chance to go back in time to interview a famous person? With this activity, your students can do just that! Divide your students into pairs, and have each pair choose a famous person related to the time period being studied. Instruct the pair to list ten interview questions on topics such as education, family life, goals, achievements, and special interests. Encourage each pair to include human-interest questions as well, such as "What was your life like when you were my age?" and "How did your achievements change you?"

Next, have each pair research its famous person to find the answers to the questions. Direct the twosome to tape-record its interview, with one student acting as interviewer and the other as the famous person. Afterward, have each pair share its interview with the class. *Lori Sammartino, Cranberry Township, PA*

A GREAT LEAP BACKWARD

What's a great way to get kids to remember history? How about if they visit history? Capitalize on kids' fascination with time travel by having students imagine that they suddenly have found themselves in the historical period they are studying. Have each student answer the following questions about his destination:

- What date did you travel back to?
- What major event is taking place?
- What useful item from the present have you taken with you?
- What can you teach the people of this period?
- What can you learn from them?
- If you could change one thing about the event taking place, what would it be? Why? How would you change it?
- Would you like to remain in the past? Why or why not?

Next, direct each student to write a narrative about her historical adventure that includes the ideas expressed in her answers. Then invite her to share her writing with the rest of the class. Betcha students really remember history they've visited! *Julia Alarie, Essex Middle School, Essex, VT*

HISTORICAL BEST-SELLERS

Do you have future prizewinning novelists in your class? Find out by challenging your students to write book proposals for historical fiction novels. First brainstorm and list on the board eight to ten major events from the time period your class is studying (see the example). After each student has selected an event, share the following guidelines for writing her book proposal:

- **Paragraph 1:** Describe the cities, places, dates, and people to be featured in your novel.
- **Paragraph 2:** Describe the main character: his or her full name, occupation, beliefs, friends, family, and physical characteristics.
- **Paragraph 3:** Summarize the plot, including its main conflicts, and historical events that affect the plot.

After sharing her completed proposal with the class, have each student design the book's jacket. Direct the student to include the title, author, and an illustration on the front of the jacket. Then, on the back, have her write a synopsis of the book that incorporates the details from her proposal. Who knows. You may have sown the seeds for the next great historical novel! *Terry Healy, Eugene Field Elementary, Manhattan, KS*

My Life as the Captain of the Monitor
by Sam Crump

Major Events of the Civil War
- problem of slavery
- slaves' escape by the Underground Railroad
- Fort Sumter attacked
- battle of the *Monitor* and *Merrimack*
- Emancipation Proclamation
- Battle of Gettysburg
- Lincoln's Gettysburg Address
- Lincoln reelected president
- Lee's surrender to Grant at Appomattox
- President Lincoln assassinated

Molly Pitcher!

THE PLAY'S THE THING!

To make history come alive for your students, let them live it! At the beginning of any history unit, divide your class into groups of four or five students each. Assign each group a historical figure or group of people, an event, or a particular time period. Tell each group that it is to gather information about its topic during the unit and plan a simple skit based on those findings. Provide time for each group to write a script for its play and gather props and costumes. Then at the end of the unit, have a Play Day. With its skits and the discussions they generate, this unique unit review is sure to get rave reviews! *Julia Alarie, Essex Middle School, Essex, VT*

CREATE-A-COLONY PROJECT

After learning about daily life in the 13 colonies, have your students create their own original settlements. First, divide students into small groups. Have each group work together to write a description of its colony, including information on the following topics:

- name, location, and size of the colony
- natural resources available
- religion(s)
- type of government: who rules? who can vote?
- towns and their locations
- foods, clothing, customs, recreation, etc.
- transportation and communication

After each group finishes its description, have it create a small mural of its colony. Then assign each group a day in which to dress up as its colony's settlers. Invite the other groups to visit that colony, view its mural, and ask questions. *Kathy Williams, Durham Elementary, Greenville, NY*

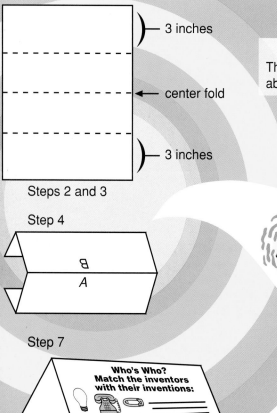

3 inches

center fold

3 inches

Steps 2 and 3

Step 4

B
A

Step 7

Who's Who?
Match the inventors with their inventions:

TEACHING TABLEGRAMS

Looking for a neat way to share what your students learn about the past? Then have them create these eye-catching tablegrams that teach readers about history and history makers. Have each student follow these steps.

1. Vertically position a sheet of white construction paper, fold it in half, and then unfold it.
2. Make a mark three inches from the top of the sheet. Fold down the top edge to the mark and make a crease.
3. Make a mark three inches from the bottom of the sheet. Fold up the bottom edge to the mark and make a crease.
4. Turn the sheet over.
5. Decide on the information you want to include on your tablegram and the format: questions-and-answer, riddle, puzzle, etc.
6. Label and illustrate section A. Then rotate the sheet and repeat for section B.
7. Stand up your completed tablegram to form a triangle. Overlap the two short tabs; then tape the tabs together at each end.

Place students' completed tablegrams on your cafeteria's tables or share them with local restaurants. Now that's a creative way to stimulate mealtime conversation! *Killeen Jensen, Tallulah Falls School, Tallulah Falls, GA*

Canada

Howdy, Neighbor!

Creative Activities for Getting Acquainted With Canada

Covering nearly four million square miles from the Atlantic to the Pacific Ocean, Canada is a land of immense variety, majestic beauty, and rich history. Get to know our vast northern neighbor with the following creative activities and reproducibles.

ideas by Simone Lepine

Good-Neighbor Venn

United States	Both	Canada
....	....	....
....	....	....
....	....	....
....	....	....
....	....	....
....	....	....
....	....	....
....	....	....

The United States and Canada have a lot in common. For one thing, they share the longest undefended border in the world—almost 5,600 miles! The two nations also share history and a similar culture and government. But they are different too. Help students spot the similarities and differences with a unique Venn diagram activity. Give each student a 12" x 18" sheet of construction paper, scissors, a glue stick, and a copy of page 46 to complete. When students have categorized the statements as directed (allow guessing), discuss the answers together using the key on page 111. Then have students glue the statements in place under the correct headings. Follow up by asking each child to write a couplet or jingle about an interesting fact he learned about Canada during the activity.

Hats Off (*and* On) to Canada!

Tip your hat to Canada's political boundaries with this living-map activity! Gather 13 baseball hats. On the front of each hat, pin a colorful index card labeled with the name of a Canadian province or territory. After selecting 13 students to wear the hats, direct the models to stand together in a designated place to show how these places are arranged on a map. Direct the hatless students to use a map (see page 47) to check the arrangement, making adjustments if necessary. Then have each hat-wearing student give her cap to a hatless classmate and repeat the activity. For an added challenge, ask each hat wearer to state a fact about Canada or her province/territory before passing the cap to a classmate.

Population Patterns

Canada's large land area makes its motto—*a mari usque ad mare* (meaning "from sea to sea")—very fitting. But why does the world's second largest country currently rank 35th in population? To help students see that the answer is tied to Canada's geography and climate, give each child a copy of page 47 and page 48 and the materials needed to complete them as directed. When students have finished their work, discuss the answers to page 48 together. Help each child conclude that Canada has a small population because much of it is difficult to inhabit due to extremely cold temperatures and harsh terrain.

Concentrating on Canada

Familiarize students with facts about Canada's provinces and territories using a Concentration game with a clearly Canadian twist! Make eight copies of the information cards on page 45 for each pair of students. Then have each twosome complete the steps below.

Preparing the cards:
1. Cut out the 16 cards. On the top part of each card, write the name of a province or territory. (Use the three extra cards in case of errors.)
2. Label the two boxes on each card with the same number.
3. Fill in each card, using a map or atlas to find the information.
4. Cut each completed card in two along its dotted line.

Playing the game:
1. Shuffle the information cards and place them facedown in a grid-like arrangement. Shuffle the label cards and place them in a different gridlike arrangement.
2. Player 1 turns over one of the information cards, reads it, and announces the province or territory he thinks it describes. Then he turns over a label card to find its match.
3. If Player 1's guess matches both faceup cards, then he keeps the cards and takes another turn.
   If Player 1's faceup cards do not match, he turns the cards facedown again and Player 2 takes a turn.
   If Player 1's faceup cards match, but his guess was different, he must turn the cards facedown again. Then Player 2 takes a turn.
4. Play continues until all cards have been correctly matched. The player with more matched pairs wins.

Province or Territory
Alberta
Label #   3
Information Card #   3

Capital city   Edmonton

Neighboring provinces or territories
British Columbia, Northwest Territiories, Saskatchewan

Neighboring U.S. state(s)
Montana

Important lakes, rivers, or oceans
Athabasca River, Peace River, Lake Athabasca

Province or Territory
Label #
Information Card #
Capital city____
Neighboring provinces or territories
Neighboring U.S. state(s)
Important lakes, rivers, or oceans

Province or Territory
Label #
Information Card #
Capital city____
Neighboring provinces or territories
Neighboring U.S. state(s)
Important lakes, rivers, or oceans

The Newest Territory

The northern part of Canada is made up of three territories: Yukon, Northwest Territories, and—as of April 1, 1999—Nunavut. *Nunavut,* which means "our land" in the Inuit language, was carved from the eastern part of the Northwest Territories. Even though it is larger than California and Alaska combined, only about 27,000 people—most of whom are Inuits—live in Nunavut. The Inuits' values and beliefs are integrated into this new territory's form of government.

After introducing these territories, divide students into three teams (one per territory). Have each team research its territory. Then draw three columns on the board, labeling one for each territory. One at a time, have each team share what it learned about its territory, while you list the findings in the appropriate column. Then post four sheets of poster board labeled as shown on a wall. Have each student draw four similar boxes on his paper. Using the columns on the board, discuss with students how the territories are alike and different. Direct students to record all responses in the appropriate boxes on their papers as you write them on the poster board sheets. The result? A graphically organized study guide for everyone!

Northwest

Yukon

All

Nunavut

The Canadian Express

Challenge students to create a display about Canada's provinces and territories that others will "ch-ch-choose" to check out! Divide students into 13 groups. Assign each group a different province or territory to research. When the research is done, share with students that Canada's two major railways, the Canadian Pacific and the Canadian National, unified the country by linking the west to the east. Next, have each group create a railroad car about its topic by following the steps below. Enlarge, color, and cut out the engine pattern provided. Then mount it on a shoebox and add wheels (see Step 8 below). Finally, arrange the groups' train cars behind the engine. All aboard!

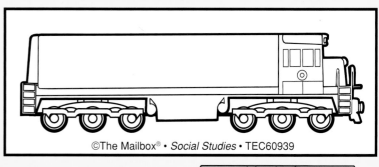

©The Mailbox® • *Social Studies* • TEC60939

Materials for each group: shoebox, colorful construction paper, crayons, scissors, tape, glue, two 3" lengths of string, 2 toilet paper tubes

Steps:

1. Decorate the outside of the shoebox to look like a train car.
2. Choose one side of the box. Across the top of this side, write the name of the province or territory.
3. Cover the box lid with paper. Label it with basic facts about the province or territory.
4. On the lid's inside, draw or glue a map of Canada *(see page 47)*. Color the province or territory.
5. Fill the shoebox with items that represent the province or territory such as a picture of Niagara Falls or a newspaper forecast showing the province's or territory's weather.
6. Cut the back corners of the lid as shown.
7. Tape the cut portion to the back of the box. Then tape one end of each piece of string to the inside of the lid and the other to the inside of the box.
8. To make the wheels, tape the toilet paper tubes to the bottom of the shoebox. Cover each tube opening with a paper circle.

Au Revoir, Quebec?

Over 80% of the seven-million-plus people in Canada's largest province of Quebec are French. Blending English and French cultures has not been easy. Over time, the French-speaking people of Quebec began to think that the only way to prevent their language and culture from declining was to make Quebec politically independent from Canada. In 1968, the *Parti Québécois* (now *Bloc Québécois*) was formed to champion this cause. Since then, this issue has been voted on—and rejected—several times. In October of 1995, it was rejected again, but this time only by a narrow margin.

Share this information with students. Then use the following questions as journal prompts or in discussion groups.

- On a blank map of Canada *(see page 47),* color Quebec red. If Quebec were to separate from Canada, what problems would this create for Canada's other provinces and territories? What effect would this have on the United States?
- How can having two national languages be helpful? What problems could be caused?
- Why is language an important part of any culture? Can a culture be kept alive and strong if its language changes? Why or why not?
- Pretend you are a French Canadian who is a member of the Bloc Québécois. Explain why you think Quebec should secede (separate) from Canada.
- Pretend you live in a province other than Quebec. Explain how you feel about Quebec's desire to separate from Canada. Why do you think it's fair or unfair? What would you say to someone who belongs to the Bloc Québécois?

Canadian Native Americans

Use this creative research project to help students discover how environment dictated the mode of abode for some Canadian Native Americans. Assign each student a different tribe to research from the five groups listed below. Direct the student to find out the approximate province/territory in which the tribe lived and in what type of home. Then have the student make a model or drawing of the dwelling.

When the projects are finished, post a large map of Canada. Have students who researched tribes from the same numbered group present their findings one after the other. Ask each student to point out on the map the approximate area where her tribe lived. After the presentations for each group have been made, talk about the building materials and styles of the homes as they relate to the physical features in the specific area(s) of Canada. To review Canada's six geographic regions (Canadian Shield, Appalachian Highlands, Great Lakes–St. Lawrence Lowlands, Interior Plains, Western Mountain Region, Arctic North), have the class identify the region in which each tribe lived.

Group 1: Plains Culture Area: Assiniboine, Blackfeet, Cree, Sioux
Group 2: Pacific Northwest Culture Area: Bella Coola, Haida, Kwakiutl, Nootka, Salish, Tsimshian
Group 3: Northeast Culture Area: Algonquin, Micmac, Huron, Iroquois, Ojibwa
Group 4: Subarctic Culture Group: Montagnais, Naskapi
Group 5: Arctic Culture Group: Inuit

Information Cards

Use with "Concentrating on Canada" on page 43.

Province or Territory	Province or Territory
Label #	Label #
Information Card #	Information Card #
Capital city _____	Capital city _____
Neighboring provinces or territories _____	Neighboring provinces or territories _____
Neighboring U.S. state(s) _____	Neighboring U.S. state(s) _____
Important lakes, rivers, or oceans _____	Important lakes, rivers, or oceans _____

Hidy Ho, Neighbor!

Monty Moose and Edgar Eagle need your help. They know that some of the statements below tell how the United States and Canada are different and that others tell what they have in common. Help these guys sort the facts by following the directions below.

Directions: Divide the paper your teacher gives you into three columns. Label the columns left to right: United States, Both, Canada. Then cut out the statements below and place them in the columns where you think they belong.

Divided into 50 states and the District of Columbia	Known as a nation of immigrants
Divided into ten provinces and three territories	Population about 30 million
One official language: English	Population more than 270 million
Two official languages: English and French	Type of government: federal republic
Second largest country in the world in area	Type of government: confederation with parliamentary democracy
Fourth largest country in the world in area	National capital: Washington, DC
Prime minister is head of government	National capital: Ottawa
President is head of government	National anthem: "O Canada"
Legislative branch is the parliament	National anthem: "The Star-Spangled Banner"
Legislative branch is the Congress	Basic unit of money: dollar
Federal parliament has a Senate and a House of Commons	Mining products: petroleum, natural gas, coal
Legislative branch has a Senate and a House of Representatives	Borders these oceans: Arctic, Atlantic, and Pacific
Senators appointed for life (or until 75 years of age)	Began as a French colony
Senators elected to six-year terms	Railways helped westward expansion
Began as British colonies	Has six time zones

Note to the teacher: Use with "Good-Neighbor Venn" on page 42. Provide each student with scissors, a glue stick, and a 12" x 18" sheet of construction paper.

Name _____

Canada

N · NE · E · SE · S · SW · W · NW

Note to the teacher: Use with "Hats Off (*and* On) to Canada!" and "Population Patterns" on page 42 and "Canada's Population Patterns" on page 48.

47

Canada's Population Patterns

Canada's land area makes it the second largest country in the world. But when it comes to population, Canada drops to 35th in the world. A lot can be learned about a country by studying its population patterns. Use a map of Canada and the data in the chart shown to help you answer the questions below.

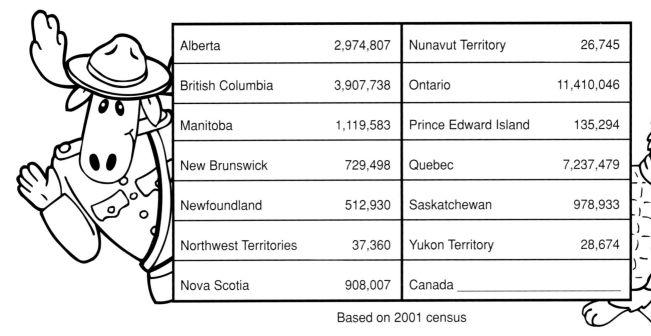

Alberta	2,974,807	Nunavut Territory	26,745
British Columbia	3,907,738	Ontario	11,410,046
Manitoba	1,119,583	Prince Edward Island	135,294
New Brunswick	729,498	Quebec	7,237,479
Newfoundland	512,930	Saskatchewan	978,933
Northwest Territories	37,360	Yukon Territory	28,674
Nova Scotia	908,007	Canada _____	

Based on 2001 census

1. Label the provinces and territories listed above on a blank political map of Canada.

2. Color the map using the key below.

   | red | Population greater than 6 million | blue | Population between 1 and 5 million | green | Population between 70,000 and 999,999 | yellow | Population less than 70,000 |

3. Look at the area colored yellow. Why do you think this area has such a low population? _____
_____

4. Add together the populations of Quebec and Ontario. _____
   Add together the populations of the 11 remaining provinces and territories. _____
   Study your map. What conclusion(s) about Canada's population can these two sums help you make? _____
_____

5. Use the data in the chart to find Canada's *total* population. Record this sum in the chart on the line provided.

6. Why do you think that most of Canada's population lives within 100 miles of its southern border?
_____
_____

Bonus Box: On the back of this page or on another sheet of paper, list the populations of the provinces and territories in order from greatest to least.

Latin America

ANCIENT CIVILIZATIONS OF LATIN AMERICA

EXPLORING THE MAYA, AZTEC, AND INCA EMPIRES

Marvel over the exceptional achievements of the Maya, Aztec, and Inca empires with the exciting activities, literature suggestions, and reproducibles that follow!

by Terry Healy, Manhattan, KS

Background Information: The Maya, Aztecs, and Incas developed some of the world's greatest civilizations. Artifacts reveal that their societies were far more advanced than other cultures at that time:

- The Maya, who lived in southern Mexico and Central America, were known for their advanced form of writing, place-value number system, and studies in astrology.
- The Aztecs set up their empire in central and southern Mexico. They were craftspeople who developed a calendar system and displayed exceptional engineering skills.
- The Incas, located in the Andes highlands of South America, excelled at architecture, built thousands of miles of roads and suspension bridges, and even terraced the land for their crops. They were also excellent potters, weavers, and metal workers.

When the Spanish arrived in the Americas, these empires began to fall. The Maya conquest began in 1500, the Aztecs fell in 1521, and the Incas in 1532.

THOSE INCREDIBLE INCAS!

Skill: Research skills

Imagine erecting structures of stone so finely cut that they needed no mortar to hold them together, or building amazing suspension and pontoon bridges using only stone tools! Help students recognize the amazing achievements of the Incas with this research project. List the topics shown below on the board. Pair students; then assign each twosome a topic to research. After each pair has researched its topic, give the students the directions on page 53 along with scissors, pinking shears, a glue stick, a fine-tip black marker, crayons, and two sheets of 9" x 12" construction paper (one light-colored and one black). Display the resulting projects on a bulletin board titled "Those Incredible Incas!"

TOPICS

- Incan Agriculture and Irrigation
- Math and Astronomy in the Incan World
- Incan Bridge Building
- Incan Medicine
- Incan Road System
- Incan Architecture

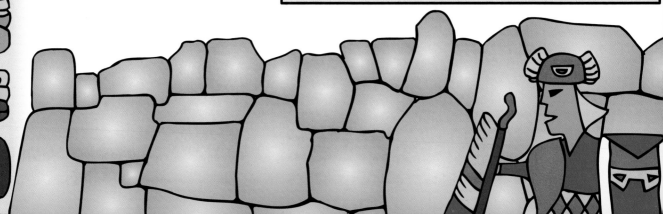

THAT'S THE WAY THE BALL BOUNCES

Skill: Writing step-by-step directions

If students want to know what a seriously competitive sport is *really* like, then tell them about the way the Maya and Aztecs played ball! Two teams of nobles in an I-shaped court would try to propel a solid rubber ball against a marker set in the center of each side of the court's walls or through vertical hoops. The players would hit the ball at high speeds from one side of the court to the other using only their hips, wrists, or elbows. Losers sometimes lost everything they had—even their lives!

For a creative-thinking challenge, have pairs of students invent a team game that's played with a small rubber ball and two hoops. Direct each pair to write a set of rules and step-by-step directions telling how to play its game. Then have the pair trade its rules and directions with another twosome. Ask each pair of students to read the directions carefully, make suggestions for revisions, and then return the directions to the authors. Collect the revised games to use during recess or at a special field day held at the end of your unit!

AZTEC ARTISANS

Skill: Following directions

If there's one thing that kept Aztec artisans busy, it was making decorative pieces of gold and silver! The Aztecs had no monetary system, so the highest classes wore these objects to symbolize their wealth. Turn students into skillful Aztec artisans by having them create golden ornaments of their own. Give each student a two-inch ball of air-drying clay, several layers of paper towels or newspapers, a dull pencil, a copy of the glyph patterns on page 54, gold or silver metallic acrylic craft paint, and a paintbrush. Direct the student to flatten and shape the clay into a ¾-inch-thick circle on the paper. Have her use the dull pencil to make a glyph from the pattern page on the circle; then have her add a repeating design around the circle's edge. Allow the clay to dry overnight. The next day have the student paint one side of the circle, allow it to dry, and then paint the other side. Use these shiny projects to enhance an existing unit display or as a springboard for writing stories about a rich Aztec who lost a golden ornament like the ones created.

TOPICS

Laughter	Clouds
Clocks	Rain
Calendars	Stars
Storms	Wheels
Games	
Fire	

THE GIFT OF MUSIC

Skill: Comparing, contrasting, and writing myths

What would the world be like without the sound of music? It wouldn't have been as great for the Aztecs because music was very important to them. Read aloud the following picture book that tells one Aztec myth about how music came to the world: *How Music Came to the World*, retold by Hal Ober. After reading the myth, have students help you map it on the board. Then list the shown topics on the board. Direct each student to write his own myth titled "How [topic] Came Into the World" to share with the class. If desired, have students compare and contrast myths written on the same topic. Or incorporate other Latin American tales into this activity using Lulu Delacre's *Golden Tales: Myths, Legends, and Folktales From Latin America*.

STRINGING ALONG

Skill: Place value

Instead of stringing students along about how the Incas kept records, use this terrific hands-on project to make it perfectly clear! The Incas kept records with a device called a *quipu,* a long cord held horizontally from which hung a series of different-colored knotted strings. To demonstrate how the Incas could have represented 364 llamas on a quipu, draw on the chalkboard the illustration shown. Point out that the set of three dots represents 300, the six dots 60, and the four dots 4. *(Note: If the numeral had been 304, leaving a space for the tens would show that there were no tens.)* Next, give each pair of students a 12-inch length of black yarn and one 18-inch length of yarn in each of the following colors: blue, red, yellow, and green. Challenge the pair to create its own version of a quipu by following the steps below. To extend this activity, have each student use crayons or colored pencils to draw pictures of quipus representing numerals of higher place values (ten thousands, hundred thousands, etc.).

Steps:

1. Partner A holds the black yarn straight by holding one end in each hand.
2. Partner B ties the blue yarn near one end of the black yarn by folding the blue yarn in half and then folding the loop over the black yarn. He then pulls the ends of the blue yarn through the loop, resulting in two lengths of blue yarn hanging from the black yarn (one for Partner A and the other for Partner B).
3. Partner B repeats Step 2 with the red, yellow, and green yarn.
4. The partners take turns making knots in the colorful yarn using this code: blue = days until next birthday, red = last two digits of birth year, yellow = pages in a class textbook, green = pages in current library book. For example, if there are 127 days until Partner A's birthday, he would make the following knots in his length of blue yarn: one knot (1 hundred, or 100) near the black yarn, two knots (2 tens, or 20) in the center, and seven knots (7 ones, or 7) near the bottom.

PICTURE THIS!

Skill: Critical thinking, art project

The Maya were the only ancient New World inhabitants to develop a true form of writing. They used picture symbols, or *hieroglyphs,* on pottery, walls, and ornaments, and in books called *codices.* The Aztecs also used hieroglyphs, but in a simpler style. Have students practice picture writing to help them recall interesting facts about the Maya and Aztecs. Give each student a sheet of light brown construction paper, colorful markers, and a copy of page 54. Direct the student to choose glyphs from page 54—along with creating some of his own design—that help him tell something about Maya or Aztec life (see the suggestions below). Then have him draw his glyphs on one side of the brown paper and write the interpretation on the flip side. Next, have him trade papers with a classmate, decipher his partner's glyphs, and flip the paper over to check. If desired, compile the papers into a class *codex* (book). Tape the papers together side to side and fold them accordion-style as shown. Add decorated front and back covers to complete the codex.

Codex of Mayan and Aztec Life

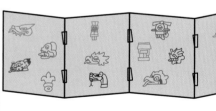

- Maya ceremonies, dances, and festivals were held in the centers of their cities.
- Only four Maya codices exist today. It is believed that hundreds more were destroyed by the Spanish.
- Priests and nobles were probably the only people who could read the Maya hieroglyphs.

- The Maya wore feather headdresses that made the wearers look like birds.
- Maya boys practiced battle skills.
- The Maya and Aztecs made dugout canoes by burning and digging out large trees.
- The Maya and Aztecs usually ate two meals per day.

INCAN ACCOMPLISHMENTS

Steps:

1. Fold the colorful paper in half width-wise. Fold it in half again as shown.
2. Make diagonal cuts across two corners of the paper as shown.
3. Unfold the paper. Use pinking shears to trim the edges of the top half of the paper. Also cut halfway down the paper, along the center crease.
4. Fold back down the two top halves to form flaps covering the bottom half of the paper.
5. Use the black marker to write "THEN" where shown. Above this label, illustrate the Incan accomplishment you researched. Then lift the flap and write a short summary of this feat on the paper below.
6. Label the right flap "NOW." Above the label, illustrate a modern version of the Incan accomplishment. Then lift the flap and summarize how the modern world accomplishes the same Incan feat today.
7. Glue the project onto the black paper.

Step 1

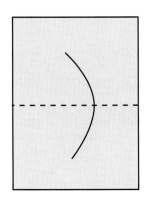 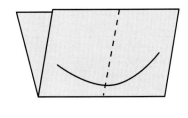

Step 2

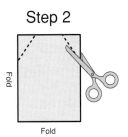

Fold

Fold

Step 3

THEN   NOW

Finished Sample

Note to the teacher: Use with "Those Incredible Incas" on page 50.

Glyph Patterns

Use with "Aztec Artisans" on page 51 and "Picture This!" on page 52.

1. crocodile
2. wind
3. house
4. lizard
5. serpent

6. death's-head
7. deer
8. rabbit
9. water
10. dog

11. monkey
12. grass
13. reed
14. ocelot
15. eagle

16. vulture
17. motion
18. flint knife
19. rain
20. flower

ANCIENT PYRAMID OF FACTS

If you were an ancient Inca, Mayan, or Aztec, you probably attended religious ceremonies that were held at a pyramid temple. Build your own pyramid to help you remember important facts about the Maya, Aztecs, and Incas!

Directions: Match each fact below with the culture it describes. Use encyclopedias to help you. Then write the fact on the corresponding pyramid wall. (Hint: Some facts will be written on more than one wall.) Next, cut out the pattern. Fold it on the dotted lines and glue where directed to form a pyramid.

Worshipped gods and goddesses
Ate cornmeal pancakes
Empire centered in Andes highlands
Used llamas to carry their goods
Had no central form of government
Spoke a language called *Quechua*

Were conquered by the Spanish
Had their capital at the city of Tenochtitlán
Empire centered in Mexico
Empire centered in southern Mexico and
      Central America

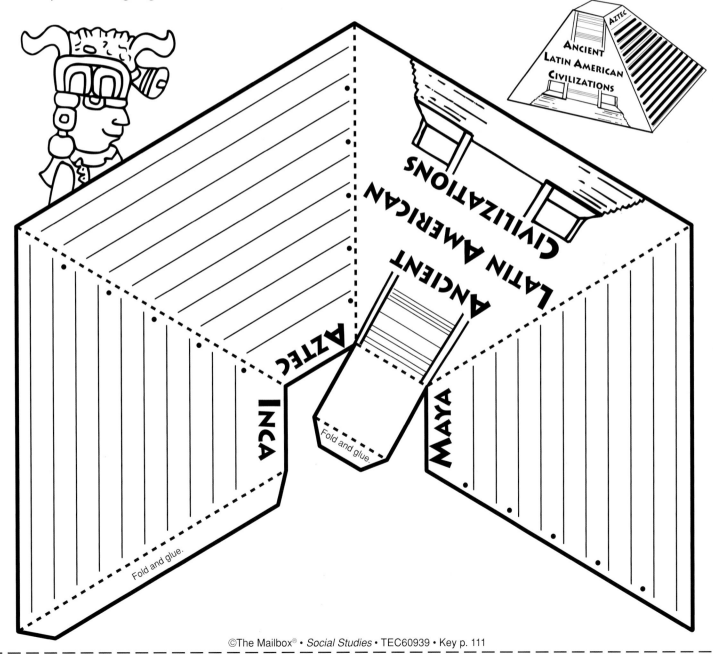

Note to the teacher: Provide students with scissors, glue, and reference materials to complete this activity.

GOIN' ON A DIG!

Much of what is known about the Maya, Aztecs, and Incas has been learned by studying artifacts from archaeological digs. Discover more about these ancient cultures and review parts of speech at the same time by taking part in a dig of your own!

Directions: Find 25 artifacts (**boldfaced** words) buried in the sentences below. List the words on the matching shapes. Here's a helpful hint: this dig consists of 8 nouns, 6 verbs, 5 adjectives, 3 adverbs, and 3 pronouns.

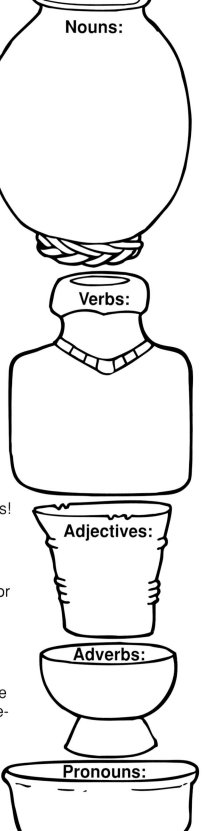

Nouns:

Verbs:

Adjectives:

Adverbs:

Pronouns:

1. The Maya thought that strapping babies to **boards** to make **their** heads longer made them more attractive.

2. The Maya **understood** the concept of zero long before it was understood in **Europe.**

3. To the Maya, Aztecs, and Incas, wearing bird feathers was a sign of wealth—like having a **fancy** car or expensive clothes today.

4. The Maya, Aztecs, and Incas placed **masks** over their mummies to protect **them** in the afterlife.

5. The Incas believed that gold **was** the "sweat of the sun." They called silver the "tears of the moon."

6. Since the Incas had no form of **writing,** studying their pottery is a **valuable** way to learn about their culture.

7. Because they had no **animals** large enough to carry heavy loads, the Maya **carried** all their goods on their backs!

8. Aztec families **raised** turkeys for food, but **they** also ate small dogs!

9. To pay taxes, all **married** Inca farmers **dutifully** spent part of their time erecting buildings or constructing roads.

10. The Incas did not have the wheel. They **patiently** rolled **huge** building stones—some weighing many tons—on large log rollers for distances as long as 18 miles!

11. The Maya and Aztecs played a game similar to the Parcheesi board game. They used beans for **dice,** stones for game pieces, and feathers and jewelry for prizes.

12. For protection, the Aztecs **built** their capital city, Tenochtitlán, in the center of a **lake.** They connected it to the mainland with removable-section bridges.

13. Each time a new baby was born, Inca families were given **more** land to farm.

14. Aztecs took steam baths in small buildings next to their homes. Each bathhouse was heated by a **fireplace.**

15. The poncho **is** a type of clothing from Inca culture that is **still** worn today.

Bonus Box: On the back of this page, list the kinds of items archaeologists find on digs.

Geography

Park It!

ACTIVITIES ON UNITED STATES REGIONS AND NATIONAL PARKS

Looking for a new way to introduce your students to our nation's regions? Then pack your teaching bag of tricks with the following activities that highlight our spectacular national parks.

with ideas by Simone Lepine

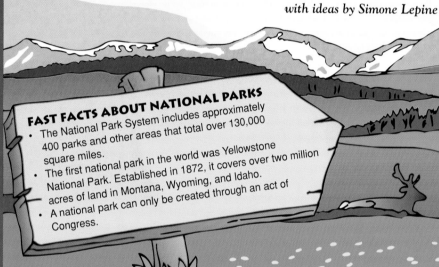

FAST FACTS ABOUT NATIONAL PARKS
- The National Park System includes approximately 400 parks and other areas that total over 130,000 square miles.
- The first national park in the world was Yellowstone National Park. Established in 1872, it covers over two million acres of land in Montana, Wyoming, and Idaho.
- A national park can only be created through an act of Congress.

BACKPACK FAST FACTS

Skills: Research, comparing and contrasting

Review important research skills on your trek through our national parks with an activity that also sharpens comparing and contrasting skills. Assign each student two parks (in two different regions) from the list on page 62. Also give each child two copies of the graphic organizer on page 61. After each student has finished researching his parks and filling out both copies of page 61, have him glue one organizer to the front of a file folder and the other to the back. Then have him open the folder and draw a large Venn diagram inside. Finally, have the student compare and contrast his two parks and fill in his diagram. As an extension, challenge each student to use an atlas to plan a route between his two parks; then have him use the scale of miles to estimate the number of miles he would cover if he hiked from one to the other.

UNPACKING MY BACKPACK

Skill: Planning and giving an oral presentation

Follow up the previous activity with a unique idea on how students can share what they learned about national parks. Have each student choose one of the two parks she researched in "Backpack Fast Facts." Then direct the student to pack her school backpack with items that represent information she learned about her park. (Provide spare backpacks for students who may need to use them. Also allow students to pack pictures or drawings as well as actual objects.) For example, a student who researched Rocky Mountain National Park might pack a sweater to represent the cold temperatures, an ice tray to represent the glaciers found there, and a plastic flower to represent the park's many wildflowers. Set aside time for each student to unpack her backpack in front of the class and share how each item relates to her park.

MYSTERY PARK

For another nifty activity to use after students have researched national parks, make one copy of page 62. Mask out the regions and list of parks on the boots; then make a class supply of the masked copy on tan construction paper. Have each student cut out his two boot patterns and label them as follows:

front of boot 1: three clues about a park he researched
back of boot 1: name of the park written lightly in pencil
front of boot 2: name of the park and the state(s) and region in which it is located

Collect the boots. Then place the boots with clues in a shoebox labeled "Clues" and the other boots in a shoebox labeled "Parks." Set the boxes at a center and encourage students to try to pair the matching boots in their free time. Or use the boots in a game between two teams. To play, draw a boot from the "Parks" box and read aloud the park's name and the state in which it is located. If a player can identify the park's region, award his team one point. For a more challenging game, draw a boot from the "Clues" box and read it aloud. If a player can identify the name of the park, award his team one point. Award two extra points if the player can name the region and state(s) in which the park is located.

MAPPIN' IT OUT

Map out a plan for practicing several important skills using the map skills reproducible on page 63. Review the U.S. regions and state postal abbreviations listed on page 62. Then give each student a copy of page 63 and crayons or colored pencils. After each child completes the page as directed, discuss the students' answers. Ask these questions: Which region has the most national parks on the map? Which regions have the least? Why do you think there are so many national parks in the West and so few in the Northeast? As an extension, divide the class into pairs. Give each twosome a copy of page 62. On this copy, have the students cross out the 14 parks listed on page 63. Then have them number the remaining parks 15–53. Finally, have the student pair label parks 15–53 by number on the map.

Grand Teton!

Snake River runs through it
Over 300,000 acres
Named after highest mountain in park

Grand Teton National Park
Wyoming
West Region

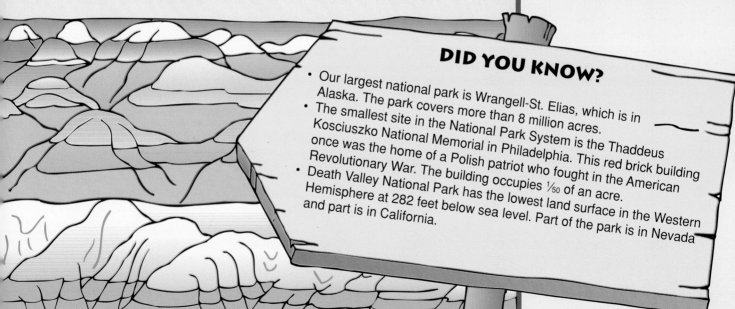

DID YOU KNOW?

- Our largest national park is Wrangell-St. Elias, which is in Alaska. The park covers more than 8 million acres.
- The smallest site in the National Park System is the Thaddeus Kosciuszko National Memorial in Philadelphia. This red brick building once was the home of a Polish patriot who fought in the American Revolutionary War. The building occupies $\frac{1}{50}$ of an acre.
- Death Valley National Park has the lowest land surface in the Western Hemisphere at 282 feet below sea level. Part of the park is in Nevada and part is in California.

PARK TREASURE HUNT

Skill: Reading for specific information

Hunt for the amazing natural treasures found in our national parks with this bulletin board activity. In advance, write each item from List A on the right on a separate white index card. Write each item from List B on a separate colored card (excluding the italicized answer). Pin the cards on a bulletin board titled "Discover the Treasures!" Next, explain to students that our parks are home to many natural treasures. Read over the items listed on the white and colored cards; then assign each student one or more parks to research. As students read, they fill in the cards with information about the treasures. For example, if a student finds out that a glacier is in his park, he writes the park's name and location on the white card labeled "glaciers." If he discovers the identity of a park that matches a colored card, he writes the park's name and location on that card.

At the end of your unit, review the treasures on the board. Then discuss these questions: Which treasures did students find most interesting? Why is it important to protect and preserve these treasures? What might happen if these treasures weren't protected?

PLACE THAT PARK!

Skill: Identifying the locations of U.S. regions and national parks

Play this fun game at the end of your unit to review the locations of U.S. regions and national parks.

To prepare:
1. After referring to page 62, write each park and the state(s) in which it is located on a separate index card. These will be called park cards.
2. Write each region's name (see page 62) on a separate colored index card. These five cards will be called region cards.
3. Write each of the five region names on a separate sheet of construction paper. Post these five sheets on your classroom walls.
4. Make a copy of your class list to use for keeping score.

To play:
1. Give each student a park card. Set the extras aside for the next round.
2. At your signal, have each student "park" himself under the sign that indicates the region in which his park is located. If desired, let students refer to the maps they completed in the "Mappin' It Out" activity on page 59.
3. Check to make sure that each student is in the correct region. Then draw and read aloud a region card. On a copy of your class list, award one point to each student in that region. Then return the card to its deck.
4. Draw one or two more region cards and award points as in Step 3.
5. To play Round 2, collect everyone's park cards and set them aside. Give each student a new park card from the extras set aside earlier. Then repeat Steps 2–4.
6. At the end of several rounds, declare the student(s) with the most (or least) points the winner.

List A *(Write each on a white index card.)*:
arches, geysers, prairies, volcanoes, deserts, islands, rivers, glaciers, Native American ruins, caves and/or caverns, petrified woods, mountains, craters, canyons, waterfalls, tundras

List B *(Write each on a colored index card, excluding the italicized answer.)*:
world's tallest trees *(Redwood)*
world's largest gorge *(Grand Canyon)*
North America's highest mountain *(Mount McKinley in Denali National Park and Preserve)*
world's largest living thing *(Sequoia and Kings Canyon)*
world's first national park *(Yellowstone)*
deepest lake in the United States *(Crater Lake)*
largest U.S. national park *(Wrangell-St. Elias)*
lowest point in western hemisphere *(Death Valley)*
world's largest known cave network *(Mammoth Cave)*
highest waterfall in North America *(Yosemite)*

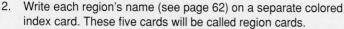

60

Name ______________________________

BACKPACK FAST FACTS

Strap on your backpack and get ready to make your mark at a national park! Research one of our country's national parks and fill in the blanks below.

____
park

____
location

____
U.S. region

Year established: ______________________________

Area (in acres): ______________________________

Important natural features: ______________________________

____

____

____

Animals: ______________________________

____

Plants: ______________________________

____

Climate: ______________________________

____

Must-see attraction at park: ______________________________

____

Cool fact: ______________________________

____

____

Researched by ______________________________

Note to the teacher: Use with "Backpack Fast Facts" on page 58.

HIKING AROUND OUR NATIONAL PARKS

(organized by region)

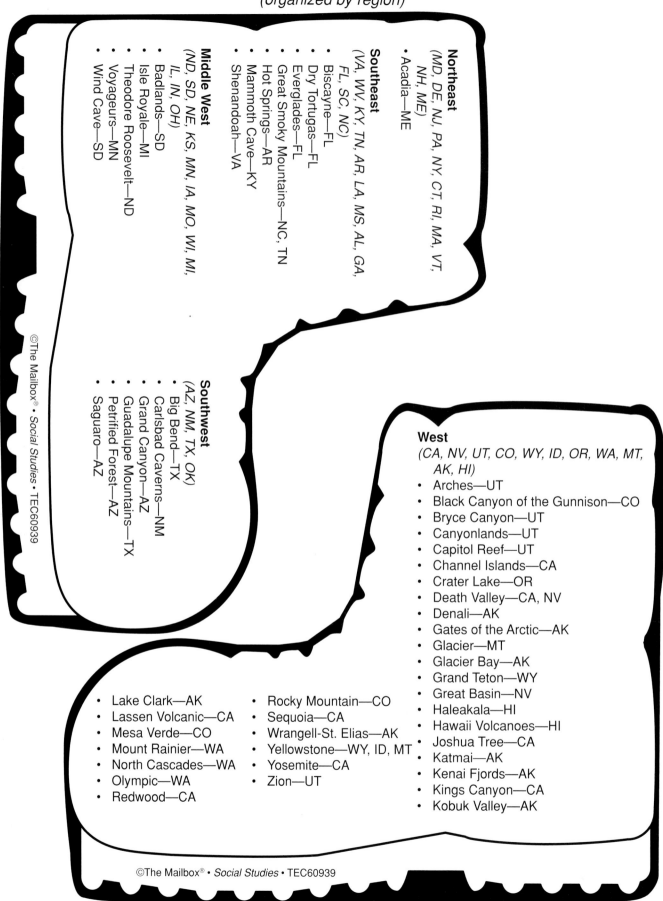

Northeast
(MD, DE, NJ, PA, NY, CT, RI, MA, VT, NH, ME)
• Acadia—ME

Southeast
(VA, WV, KY, TN, AR, LA, MS, AL, GA, FL, SC, NC)
• Biscayne—FL
• Dry Tortugas—FL
• Everglades—FL
• Great Smoky Mountains—NC, TN
• Hot Springs—AR
• Mammoth Cave—KY
• Shenandoah—VA

Middle West
(ND, SD, NE, KS, MN, IA, MO, WI, MI, IL, IN, OH)
• Badlands—SD
• Isle Royale—MI
• Theodore Roosevelt—ND
• Voyageurs—MN
• Wind Cave—SD

Southwest
(AZ, NM, TX, OK)
• Big Bend—TX
• Carlsbad Caverns—NM
• Grand Canyon—AZ
• Guadalupe Mountains—TX
• Petrified Forest—AZ
• Saguaro—AZ

West
(CA, NV, UT, CO, WY, ID, OR, WA, MT, AK, HI)
• Arches—UT
• Black Canyon of the Gunnison—CO
• Bryce Canyon—UT
• Canyonlands—UT
• Capitol Reef—UT
• Channel Islands—CA
• Crater Lake—OR
• Death Valley—CA, NV
• Denali—AK
• Gates of the Arctic—AK
• Glacier—MT
• Glacier Bay—AK
• Grand Teton—WY
• Great Basin—NV
• Haleakala—HI
• Hawaii Volcanoes—HI
• Joshua Tree—CA
• Katmai—AK
• Kenai Fjords—AK
• Kings Canyon—CA
• Kobuk Valley—AK
• Lake Clark—AK
• Lassen Volcanic—CA
• Mesa Verde—CO
• Mount Rainier—WA
• North Cascades—WA
• Olympic—WA
• Redwood—CA
• Rocky Mountain—CO
• Sequoia—CA
• Wrangell-St. Elias—AK
• Yellowstone—WY, ID, MT
• Yosemite—CA
• Zion—UT

Note to the teacher: Use with "Backpack Fast Facts" on page 58, "Mystery Park" and "Mappin' It Out" on page 59, and "Place That Park!" on page 60.

PARK IT IN THE USA!

The numbers on the map show the locations of 14 national parks in the United States. Use the state abbreviations to match each number to the correct park. Write the numbers in the blanks. Then follow the directions in the box below.

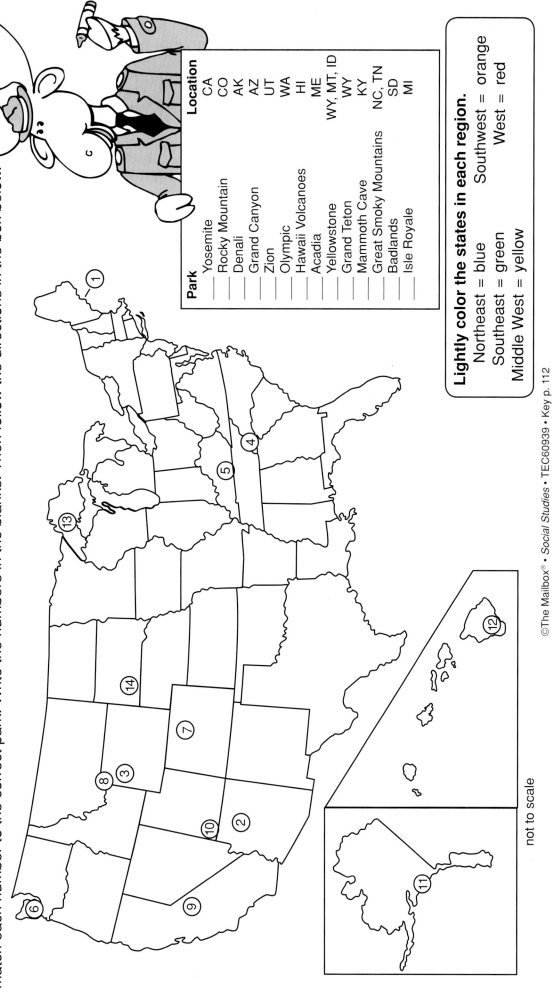

Park	Location
___ Yosemite	CA
___ Rocky Mountain	CO
___ Denali	AK
___ Grand Canyon	AZ
___ Zion	UT
___ Olympic	WA
___ Hawaii Volcanoes	HI
___ Acadia	ME
___ Yellowstone	WY, MT, ID
___ Grand Teton	WY
___ Mammoth Cave	KY
___ Great Smoky Mountains	NC, TN
___ Badlands	SD
___ Isle Royale	MI

Lightly color the states in each region.
Northeast = blue   Southwest = orange
Southeast = green   West = red
Middle West = yellow

not to scale

©The Mailbox® • *Social Studies* • TEC60939 • Key p. 112

Note to the teacher: Use with "Mappin' It Out" on page 59. Students will need crayons or colored pencils to complete this activity. Review state postal abbreviations before introducing the map to students. If desired, have students label the states with their abbreviations before having them complete the coloring activity in the box.

Jazzin' Up Geography!

Need some new ways to teach geography skills, themes, and standards?
Then try this noteworthy ensemble of cool activities and reproducibles!

ideas by Simone Lepine, Fayetteville, NY

Globe-Trottin' It!

Concept: Location
Skill: Latitude and longitude

Put pizzazz into latitude and longitude practice with a game that requires a little globe-trotting! Pair students; then give each twosome a world political map labeled with latitude and longitude lines, unlined paper, a die, two different crayons, scissors, and a copy of page 67. Direct the pair to label its paper with headings, as shown below, and then cut the cards apart, shuffle them, and stack them in a latitude pile and a longitude pile. Guide students through the steps below.

Steps:
1. Player 1 draws a latitude card and rolls the die. If the roll is even, he records the latitude on his chart as degrees *north;* if odd, as degrees *south.* (No rolling of the die is needed for "0°" cards.) Then he puts the card on the bottom of the pile.
2. Player 1 repeats Step 1, this time drawing a card from the longitude pile. If the roll is even, the longitude is recorded as degrees *east;* if *odd,* as degrees *west.* If the player draws a Wild Card, he chooses any longitude desired.
3. Player 1 uses his crayon to plot a point on the map at the coordinates listed on his chart. Then he records the name of the country or body of water.
4. Player 2 takes a turn by following Steps 1–3.
5. Play continues until both players have marked ten locations on the map. Declare the player who plots more points on *different* continents and bodies of water the winner.

Jenna			Kevin		
Latitude	Longitude	Place	Latitude	Longitude	Place
80°N	40°W	Greenland	0°	14°E	Congo
20°N	100°W	Mexico	20°S	140°E	Australia

Todd

If Vermont is east of me,
Pennsylvania is south of me,
Canada is north of me, and
Lake Erie is west of me,
who am I?

New York

You've Met My Neighbors—
Now Who Am I?

Concept: Location
Skill: Cardinal directions

Tune students in to relative location with this fast-paced game. Give each child an index card labeled with a different country or state. Have the student sign the back of his card; then have him use a map (or atlas) and cardinal directions to add clues that mention the location's neighbors. Collect the completed cards.

To play, divide students into two teams. Choose a card and read its clues to Team 1. (Explain that the clues' writer should not participate in that round.) If Team 1 identifies the location correctly, award it one point. If Team 1 is wrong, allow Team 2 to guess. Then read the next card's clues to Team 2. Continue until all the places have been guessed. Declare the team with more points the winner.

On the Lookout for Landforms

Concept: Place
Skill: Distinguishing different physical landforms

Pack your bags and get ready to send students on a globe-spanning search for landforms! Assign each child a term from the list below. Direct her to create a poster that includes a definition and illustration of the term, plus a world map that shows several places where the landform can be found. Display the completed posters.

Next, divide students into groups of four. Give each group a reproducible political map and any four of the terms listed. Challenge each group to use the displayed posters to draw a route on its map for tourists who want to visit the four landforms. If desired, have the group include a written itinerary. As each group shares its map, have different group members point out the posters they used. Watch out—travel bugs might begin to bite!

Oasis

Definition: _____

Geography terms: bay, canyon, cape, channel, delta, desert, fjord, glacier, gulf, harbor, island, isthmus, lake, mesa, mountain, mountain range, oasis, peninsula, plain, plateau, river, strait, swamp, tributary, valley, volcano

Wish You Were Here!

Concept: Region
Skill: Comparing and contrasting

Fine-tune geography skills with an activity that lets students fantasize about a dream vacation. First, obtain several copies of four different vacation brochures from a local travel agency. Place the four sets of brochures at a center along with copies of page 68. As a classwork or free-time activity, have each student study the four brochures, complete the reproducible as directed, and then share the reasons for her choices. Extend the activity by tallying students' top getaway choices on the board. Then have each child use the data to create a graph titled "Great Getaways."

Picture	Description	Effects on Humans	Effects on Environment
	Golden Gate Bridge	Easier to travel	Car exhaust increases air pollution
	Hiking the Appalachian Trail	Relaxation, seeing the beauty of nature	Litter, possible forest fires

People + Environment

Concept: Human-environment interaction
Skill: Drawing conclusions

Help students understand the give-and-take relationship that exists between humans and the environment with this group activity. First, ask students to help you collect a class supply of pictures showing various ways—both positive and negative—in which people interact with or react to their environment, such as hiking, farming, bulldozing, lumbering, wearing coats and hats, and using air conditioners and heaters. Next, divide students into groups of four. Give each group at least four different pictures, a sheet of poster board, a glue stick, and markers. Have each group discuss how the activity in each picture affects both the environment and humans. Then have the group record its conclusions on a poster similar to the one shown. After the posters have been shared with the class, display them on a bulletin board.

The World Shopping Network

Concept: Movement
Skills: Sorting, graphing

Use this simple activity to help students understand how common it is to own items manufactured all over the world. With the class, brainstorm several products that originate in different parts of the United States or the world (apples from Washington, lobsters from Maine, televisions from Japan, cars from Germany, etc.). Next, give each child 20 index cards. For homework, have him identify items in his home that come from places other than his hometown and list each one and its place of origin on a card.

When all the cards have been returned, divide students into groups of six. Instruct group members to share their cards with one another and then sort them—by state, region, or country—according to where the items were grown or manufactured. Then have each group create a bar graph of its data to share with the class. Also have the students suggest how the products were transported to their homes.

Think I'll truck on down from Cincinnati to Atlanta on I-75.

Keep On Truckin'!

Concept: Movement
Skill: Reading a map

How *does* a Maine lobster make its way to a dinner table in Arizona? To help students get a better understanding of how goods are transported from one part of North America to another, obtain one U.S. road map for every four students. Divide students into groups of four and distribute the maps. Explain that an *interstate highway* is part of a system of roadways that connect most major cities in the United States. Have students use their map keys to find the interstate highway symbol. Then call out two major cities. Have each group find and record both the interstate highway(s) and direction(s) in which a truck would travel if it were going from city A to city B. Call on one group to share its answer. After confirming the correct route(s), call out two different cities. As an extra challenge, have students agree on an average posted speed limit for the interstates. Then have each group estimate the total distance and time it would take a truck to travel between the two cities.

Latitude 0° Equator	Latitude 10° (N/S)	Latitude 20° (N/S)	Latitude 30° (N/S)	Latitude 40° (N/S)
Latitude 50° (N/S)	Latitude 60° (N/S)	Latitude 70° (N/S)	Latitude 80° (N/S)	Latitude 90° (N/S)
Longitude 0° Prime Meridian	Longitude 10° (E/W)	Longitude 20° (E/W)	Longitude 30° (E/W)	Longitude 40° (E/W)
Longitude 50° (E/W)	Longitude 60° (E/W)	Longitude 70° (E/W)	Longitude 80° (E/W)	Longitude 90° (E/W)
Longitude 100° (E/W)	Longitude 110° (E/W)	Longitude 120° (E/W)	Longitude 130° (E/W)	Longitude 140° (E/W)
Longitude 150° (E/W)	Longitude 160° (E/W)	Longitude 170° (E/W)	Longitude 180° (E/W)	Longitude WILD CARD!

I'm Dreamin' of a Great Getaway!

Imagine going to places you've always dreamed of visiting! But where would you go first? Next? To help you decide, use the brochures your teacher gives you to fill in the suitcases below. Next, write a number 1–4 on each luggage tag to show the order in which you'd like to visit these places. Then complete your vacation getaway plans by answering the questions below on another sheet of paper.

Place: _____
Natural attractions: _____
_____
_____
Other attractions: _____
_____
_____
Climate: _____
_____

Place: _____
Natural attractions: _____
_____
_____
Other attractions: _____
_____
_____
Climate: _____
_____

Place: _____
Natural attractions: _____
_____
_____
Other attractions: _____
_____
_____
Climate: _____
_____

Place: _____
Natural attractions: _____
_____
_____
Other attractions: _____
_____
_____
Climate: _____
_____

1. Look back at the numbers on the luggage tags showing the order in which you wish to visit the places above. Why do you want to visit those places in that order?

2. How is your first vacation choice *different* from the area where you live? How is it the *same?*

3. What are the major differences between your second and third vacation choices?

4. What things could you see and do at your first vacation choice that you couldn't at the fourth?

Stormin' Into September
Activities to Improve Latitude and Longitude Skills

Why is September a great time to target your students' latitude and longitude skills? Because it's also the peak month of hurricane season in the Atlantic. Merge these two hot topics with the following creative activities for a combination that's a full-blown winner!

with ideas by Kimberly A. Minafo

Latitude and Longitude Language

Skill: Understanding map skills terminology

Familiarize students with the language of latitude and longitude using the following group activity. Follow these steps:

1. Write this sentence on the board: "These terms name things that help us l_____ p_____."
2. List these words below the sentence: *meridian, longitude, hemisphere, parallel, equator, landform, prime meridian, tsunami, latitude, metropolis, taiga, precipitation.* Announce that five of the words don't belong in the list.
3. Divide the class into small groups. Challenge each group to use a social studies textbook's glossary and a dictionary to find the unrelated terms and determine what the remaining words have in common *(they all have to do with a globe and locating places)*. Also challenge the group to fill in the sentence's blanks. Allow ten to 15 minutes for students to complete this step.
4. Poll groups to find out which words students think don't belong *(taiga, landform, tsunami, metropolis, precipitation)*. Cross out these terms. Then discuss the meanings of the words that remain.
5. Ask groups to share the words they believe complete the sentence. Write the correct words in the blanks *(locate places)*.

Follow up this discussion with the hands-on art project described on the right.

These terms name things that help us <u>locate places</u>.

meridian	longitude
hemisphere	parallel
equator	~~landform~~
prime meridian	~~tsunami~~
latitude	~~metropolis~~
~~taiga~~	~~precipitation~~

Hurricane Hemispheres

Skills: Locating continents and oceans, researching

Hurricanes occur in the North Atlantic Ocean and the northeastern North Pacific Ocean. In the western Pacific Ocean, these mighty storms are called *typhoons,* while in the Indian Ocean, they're called *cyclones.* Have students pinpoint the locations of a few famous hurricanes from around the world on their own globe models.

Materials for each student: 2 white paper plates, black marker, markers or crayons, length of string, stapler, tape, access to maps and atlases, tinsel or colorful shredded paper (optional), glue (optional)

Steps:

1. Use a black marker to draw the Western Hemisphere on the back of one paper plate. Draw the Eastern Hemisphere on the back of the other plate. Label the oceans and continents on both plates.
2. Research in almanacs, on the Internet, or in other sources to find the names and dates of four different hurricanes (at least one for each of the two hemispheres on the plates). Write the name and date of each hurricane on the appropriate hemisphere to show its point of origin or an area in which it caused great destruction.
3. Color the land green and the water areas blue on both plates.
4. To make a hanger, tape one end of the string inside one plate. If desired, glue tinsel around the edges of the plate.
5. Staple the plates together as shown.

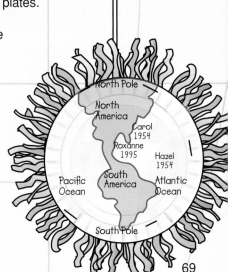

Hurricane Hunt

How do we find out how strong a hurricane is or the direction in which it's traveling? Brave Air Force pilots called the Hurricane Hunters fly directly into the eye of a hurricane to gather information for the National Hurricane Center.

Invite students to take an imaginary trip with the Hurricane Hunters by playing the following latitude and longitude game. Give each pair of students the materials listed. Direct the students in each pair to sit in desks across from each other. Stand a file folder between the twosome so students can't see each other's maps. Explain that the map shows a hurricane-prone area. Then have students follow these steps.

Materials for each student: copy of page 71, crayon, large sticky note, pencil

Steps for playing:
1. Each player colors in five grid boxes on his map. Each box represents a Hurricane Hunter airplane.
2. Player 1 calls out a specific pair of coordinates on the map, such as "22°N, 96°W." He lists these coordinates on his sticky note so he won't repeat them later. (Note: No coordinates may fall on a marked grid line.)
3. If the coordinates fall within one of Player 2's colored boxes, Player 2 circles that box and announces, "You've located one Hurricane Hunter airplane." If the coordinates do not fall within a colored box, Player 2 announces, "Miss."
4. Player 2 repeats Steps 2 and 3.
5. Play continues until one player has located all five of his opponent's planes, indicating that all hurricane information has been collected and sent to the hurricane center.

Passports, Please

A hurricane certainly doesn't wait for an invitation to drop in anywhere around the globe. But if it did, it might need a passport! Practice latitude and longitude by having students make passports for a few powerful storms. First, give each student the materials listed. Display the chart shown. Explain to students that the chart lists five imaginary hurricanes and the latitude and longitude coordinates of the places in their paths (see the key). After each student completes the steps given, have him swap passports with a partner. Direct partners to check each other's passports to see whether places have been correctly identified.

Materials: 4 half sheets of copy paper; stapler; crayons, markers, or colored pencils; access to a world map

Steps:
1. Staple the four half sheets of paper together to make a booklet. Decorate the booklet cover to resemble a passport (see the example).
2. Choose one hurricane from the list. Write each pair of coordinates at the top of a separate booklet page.
3. Look at a world map to find the place that is located at the first page's coordinates. "Stamp" the page by labeling it with the name of the place. Add a picture to represent the place (for example, a drawing of the state or country or its flag).
4. Repeat Step 3 for the other booklet pages.

Hurricane	Coordinates
Riley	(33°N, 81°W), (35°N, 79°W), (37°N, 78°W)
Tasha	(29°N, 81°W), (32°N, 84°W), (32°N, 86°W)
Ezmerelda	(31°N, 89°W), (32°N, 93°W), (32°N, 96°W)
Jimmy	(18°N, 77°W), (21°N, 87°W), (28°N, 97°W)
Alex	(39°N, 76°W), (39°N, 74°W), (42°N, 74°W)

Key
Riley:
South Carolina, North Carolina, Virginia
Tasha:
Florida, Georgia, Alabama
Ezmerelda:
Mississippi, Louisiana, Texas
Jimmy:
Jamaica, Mexico, Texas
Alex:
Delaware, New Jersey, New York

Name

Hurricane Hunt

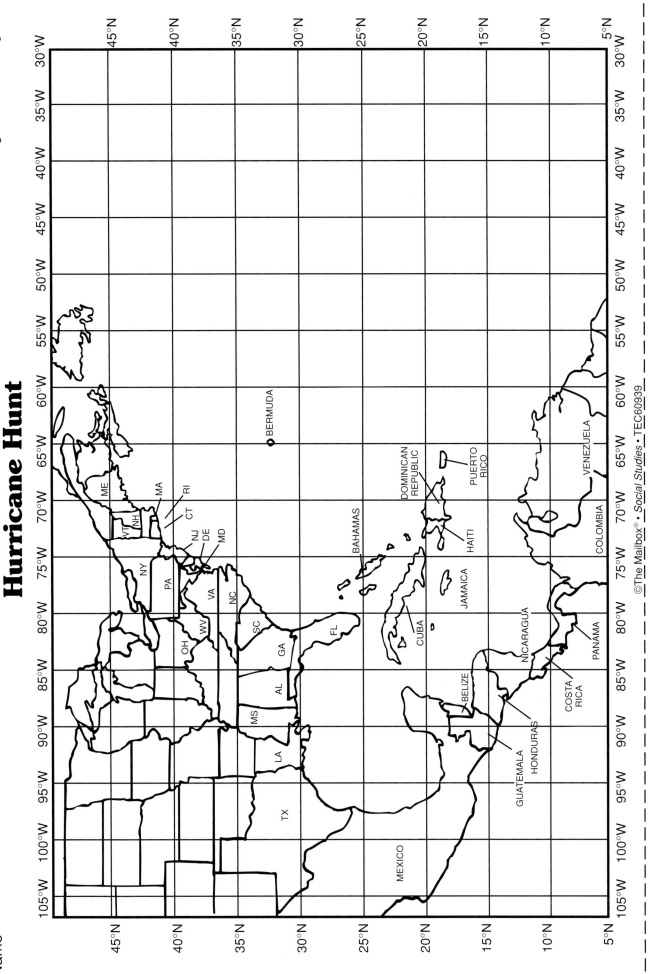

Note to the teacher:: Use with "Hurricane Hunt" on page 70.

Live From the American Landscape!

Investigating U.S. Landforms and Other Natural Features

Whether you're looking for spacious skies, amber waves of grain, purple mountain majesties, or fruited plains, America the beautiful seems to have them all. Investigate the landforms and other natural features that dot our country's landscape with the following activities.

with ideas by Simone Lepine
Gillette Road Middle School, Cicero, NY

"Land-o"
Skill: Learning geographical terms

Make learning geography terms anything but boring with this variation of bingo. Give each student one of the terms below and a 12" x 18" sheet of art paper. Have the student make a poster that includes the word and its definition, an illustration, and one real-life example. After students share their work, display the posters on a bulletin board.

Next, make a class supply of a bingo card similar to the one shown. Cover the display with a large piece of bulletin board paper; then display a transparency of the terms. Direct each student to randomly label each space on his card with one of the words. When the boards are ready, give each student a handful of markers. Read aloud a definition, checking off the term on your own copy of the list. Have each student who has the matching word on his card cover it with a marker. Continue until one child covers five words in a row in any direction and yells "Land-o!" If he has covered the correct words, award him a small prize. Then continue playing for several more rounds.

L	A	N	D-O	
		FREE		

Terms

archipelago	divide	mountain
basin	dune	mountain range
bay	fjord	peak
butte	foothill	peninsula
canyon	glacier	plain
cape	gorge	plateau
cliff	hill	prairie
crevasse	isthmus	strait
delta	lake	valley
desert	mesa	volcano

Make a Model
Skill: Identifying landforms and other natural features

Who says play dough is just for little kids? Not in this game, which challenges students to build models of natural features. Let students help you create a batch of dough using the recipe shown. Then follow these steps:

1. Divide the class into teams of three or four.
2. Give each team a laminated sheet of construction paper or a plastic placemat and a large lump of dough.
3. Write a term from the list on this page on the board. Set a timer for one minute. Then challenge Team 1 to use the dough to construct a model of the natural feature on the team's mat.
4. When time is up, award Team 1 five points for a correct model and three additional points if the team can correctly define the term. If the model is incorrect, reset the timer and challenge Team 2 to construct the model.
5. Continue until time is up or all words are used. Declare the team with the most points at the end of the game the winner.

No-Cook Modeling Dough

Mix four cups flour, two cups salt, and one-fourth cup vegetable oil. Add water and food coloring until dough is desired consistency and color.

Carlsbad Caverns

_____
_____
_____
_____

Time to Change
Skills: Researching, completing a chart

Once students learn about the variety of natural features found in the United States, they may ask, "But how did they get here?" Challenge them to answer that question themselves with this activity. First, explain that many of today's landforms were formed by the process of erosion. Erosion breaks rock and soil loose from the land at one place and moves it to another. Wind, ice, water, and temperature changes are just some of the agents of erosion. Further explain that some landforms were formed by forces related to the movement of the earth's tectonic plates, which can cause volcanoes and earthquakes.

After this discussion, divide the class into pairs. Have each twosome research one of the landforms shown to find out how it was formed. Next, have the pair decorate a large yellow or gray construction paper circle with an illustration of its landform (hand-drawn or cut from a magazine) and an explanation of how it was formed. Display the cutouts on a bulletin board titled "Time to Change."

Landforms

Appalachian Mountains	Great Lakes
Badlands	Great Sand Dunes
Bryce Canyon	Hawaiian Islands
Carlsbad Caverns	Mount Shasta
Cascade Range	Niagara Falls
Death Valley	Outer Banks
Everglades	Rocky Mountains
Grand Canyon	Teton Mountains

How Low (or High) Can You Go?
Skill: Understanding differences in elevation

Get students out of their seats and on their feet with this lively activity on elevation! Label ten 9" x 12" sheets of paper with the labels in the diagram below (one per sheet). Also give each student an enlarged copy of the diagram. Explain to students that the diagram—called a _cross section_—shows how the United States might look if cut across from east to west. The labels indicate the approximate locations and elevations of some prominent physical features.

After discussing the cross section, ask ten students to stand at the front of the classroom. Randomly give a poster to each child. Then challenge the seated classmates to direct the standing students so that they arrange themselves according to the cross section. After this is done successfully, have the two ocean students lie flat on the floor. Instruct the standing students to show their different elevations by changing their heights in some way. For example, the Rocky Mountains student might stand on a chair while the Great Basin child kneels. After the first group completes its cross section, have these students swap places with seated classmates. Then see whether the new students can arrange themselves without assistance.

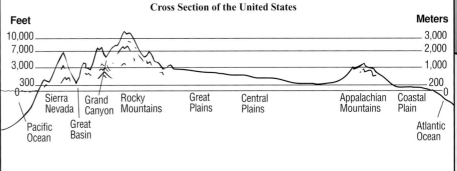

Cross Section of the United States

Feet		Meters
10,000		3,000
7,000		2,000
3,000		1,000
300		200
0		0

Sierra Nevada, Grand Canyon, Rocky Mountains, Great Plains, Central Plains, Appalachian Mountains, Coastal Plain

Pacific Ocean, Great Basin, Atlantic Ocean

Tops in Topography
Skills: Creating bar graphs, researching

Work a little math and research skills practice into your study of U.S. natural features! Post a transparency of the figures shown. Then have students use the figures to complete the following activities:

• For each set of data, create a bar graph that illustrates the differences between the five features.
• Label the features listed on a blank U.S. map (see page 76).
• Research any two of the features listed. Write a paragraph or design a poster that compares and contrasts the features.
• Research to find out the top five features in each category worldwide.
• Write a series of math word problems based on the data for your classmates to solve.

Highest U.S. Mountains	
Mt. McKinley, AK	20,320 ft.
Mt. Whitney, CA	14,494 ft.
Mt. Elbert, CO	14,433 ft.
Mt. Rainier, WA	14,410 ft.
Gannett Peak, WY	13,804 ft.

Great Lakes	
Lake Superior	31,820 sq. mi.
Lake Huron	23,010 sq. mi.
Lake Michigan	22,400 sq. mi.
Lake Erie	9,940 sq. mi.
Lake Ontario	7,540 sq. mi.

Longest U.S. Rivers	
Missouri	2,540 mi.
Mississippi	2,340 mi.
Yukon	1,979 mi.
Rio Grande	1,885 mi.
Arkansas	1,396 mi.

Hot, Cold, Wet, or Dry?
Skill: Understanding the relationship between land and climate

Help your students understand how land features affect climate with the reproducibles on pages 75 and 76. Before students complete the pages, discuss these concepts:

• As air rises, it becomes colder and less able to hold much moisture. Therefore, when air that rises to go over a mountain becomes colder, it may lose much of its moisture. This means that a place located on a mountain will generally have a wetter, cooler climate than a place at a lower elevation.
• Mountains can affect the climate of nearby lowland areas. For example, the lowlands that lie west of the Cascades receive heavy precipitation from winds that blow in from the Pacific Ocean. But by the time these moisture-laden winds pass over the Cascades, they've lost most of their moisture. That leaves the area east of the Cascades dry.
• Areas nearer the equator receive more direct sun rays. They are therefore warmer than areas that aren't as close to the equator.

American Landscape Legends
Skills: Writing a legend, researching

Did you know that Niagara Falls was created by Paul Bunyan, who was only trying to give his messy daughter a much-needed shower? Many stories about this legendary hero attempt to explain how he created some of America's most famous natural features. Ask your media specialist to help you gather some books or stories about Paul Bunyan. Share the books with your class. Then have each student research one of the features listed below (and on page 73) and write a legend that explains how it came into existence. At the end of the story, have the student include a brief epilogue that cites real facts about the feature. Bind the stories, along with student-drawn illustrations, in a class book titled "American Landscape Legends."

Natural Features

Bonneville Salt Flats	Mississippi River
Crater Lake	Mojave Desert
Devils Tower	Monument Valley
Great Salt Lake	Mount McKinley
Great Smoky Mountains	Mount Saint Helens

74

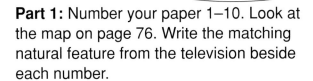

This Just In!

The climate and natural features around the United States are as different as our country is big. More at 11:00! (But don't wait till then! Find out for yourself by completing the activities below.)

Part 1: Number your paper 1–10. Look at the map on page 76. Write the matching natural feature from the television beside each number.

Part 2: Below are five lists related to climate. Underline each city's name on the map with a crayon, marker, or colored pencil as directed. CAREFUL, a few cities will need to be underlined with two different colors.

Alaska Range	Gulf of Mexico
Appalachian Mountains	Mississippi River
Atlantic Ocean	Pacific Ocean
Cascade Range	Rocky Mountains
Great Lakes	Sierra Nevada

 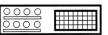

Top Five Driest U.S. Cities
average yearly precipitation
(brown)

1. Yuma, AZ (2.65")
2. Las Vegas, NV (4.19")
3. Bishop, CA (5.61")
4. Bakersfield, CA (5.72")
5. Phoenix, AZ (7.11")

Top Five Wettest U.S. Cities
average yearly precipitation
(blue)

1. Quillayute, WA (105.18")
2. Astoria, OR (66.40")
3. Tallahassee, FL (65.71")
4. Mobile, AL (63.96")
5. Pensacola, FL (62.25")

Top Five Snowiest U.S. Cities
average yearly snowfall
(orange)

1. Blue Canyon, CA (240.8")
2. Marquette, MI (129.2")
3. Sault Ste. Marie, MI (116.1")
4. Syracuse, NY (114.0")
5. Caribou, ME (110.0")

Top Five Hottest U.S. Cities
average temperature
(red)

1. Key West, FL (77.7°F)
2. Miami, FL (75.6°F)
3. West Palm Beach, FL (74.6°F)
4. Fort Myers, FL (73.9°F)
5. Yuma, AZ (73.9°F)

Top Five Coldest U.S. Cities
average temperature
(yellow)

1. International Falls, MN (36.4°F)
2. Duluth, MN (38.2°F)
3. Caribou, ME (38.9°F)
4. Marquette, MI (39.2°F)
5. Sault Ste. Marie, MI (39.7°F)

Part 3: Use the map and reference books to answer these questions on a separate sheet of paper.
1. How is it possible for California to have both very dry and very snowy cities?
2. How do mountains affect the climate in Las Vegas, Nevada?
3. What do all of the wettest cities have in common in terms of location?
4. What do the hottest cities have in common in terms of location? The coldest cities?

Note to the teacher: Use this page with "Hot, Cold, Wet, or Dry?" on page 74 and the reproducible on page 76. Provide students with access to encyclopedias or other references.

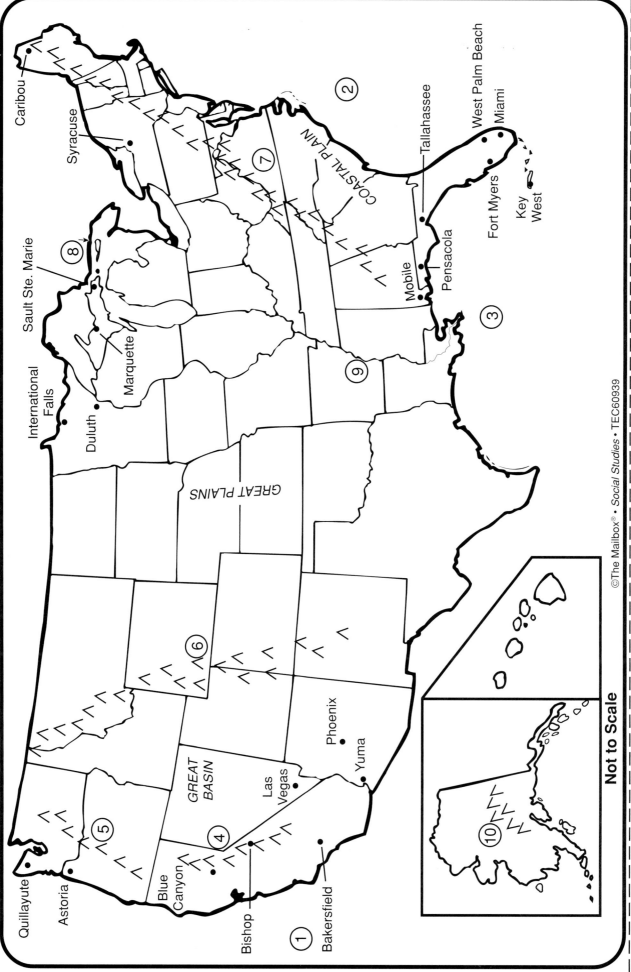

Not to Scale

©The Mailbox® • Social Studies • TEC60939

Note to the teacher: Use this page with "Tops in Topography" and "Hot, Cold, Wet, or Dry?" on page 74. To complete this map for "Hot, Cold, Wet, or Dry?" on page 75, each student will need a copy of page 75 and crayons, colored pencils, or fine-tip markers in these colors: brown, blue, orange, yellow, red.

This Must Be the Place!
Creative Map Activities That Really Hit the Spot

On the lookout for mapping activities that will keep intermediate kids tuned in? Just point your compass in the direction of the following fun-filled, hands-on learning ideas!

by Julia Alarie

Information, Please!
Skill: Reading a map

How much knowledge do your students already have about maps? Find out by presenting them with this challenge! Divide your class into groups of three or four students each, and have each group choose a recorder. Provide each group with a copy of the same map (political, physical, products/natural resources, or population density) of an area you're about to study. Also give each group a large sheet of paper. Instruct the students in each group to brainstorm everything they learn by studying the map. Have the recorder jot down each observation. After about ten minutes, compare all the information generated and check it for accuracy. Discuss how students discovered each fact. Proclaim the group with the most accurate information the "Official Class Cartographers"!

More Information, Please!
Skill: Comparing information on different kinds of maps

Extend the activity in "Information, Please!" by giving each group a different kind of map of the same area. For example, provide one group with a population density map, another with a climate regions map, a third with a products or natural resources map, a fourth with a physical features map, and a fifth with a political map. Have the students in each group brainstorm all the information they can gather from studying their map. Check each group's observations for accuracy. Then compare the kinds of information acquired from the different maps. Lead the students to draw conclusions about the relationships among the facts gathered. For example: How does elevation affect population density? How is climate related to kinds of products? What natural features form boundaries? Now that's a booty of solid-gold learning!

Welcome to Rectanguland!
Skill: Using map symbols, following directions

Provide students with plenty of practice using map symbols and following directions with the reproducible on page 80. First, go over the directions with students. Stress that they should complete steps 1 and 2 before beginning their maps. When all the maps are finished, compare and discuss the results; then have students color their finished products. Display the marvelous maps on a bulletin board titled "Rectanguland: You *Can* Get There From Here!"

Maps in the News
Skill: Current events, geography

What's often buried between the pages of today's news? Maps, mateys! Reserve a section of a wall or bulletin board on which to create a "Maps in the News" collage. Encourage students to be on the lookout for maps that accompany articles in newspapers and newsmagazines. Post the maps—along with their captions and the articles—as an ongoing reminder that maps are a big part of our everyday lives. In addition, post the following questions on the board to spark classroom discussions:

- What type of map is shown? (political, physical, population, products, etc.)
- What is the purpose of the map?
- On what continent does the news story take place? In what country? In which state?
- What type of story does the map accompany? (politics, culture, climate, disaster, etc.)
- List three facts you can learn from the map.

Can Someone Give Me Directions?
Skill: Cardinal directions

Using wall-mounted maps ("north is up, south is down") to teach cardinal directions is often confusing for students. To help them better understand the true cardinal directions, use colored masking tape to make a compass rose right on your classroom floor. First, get students' input to help you determine the actual directions; then make the compass rose accordingly. Since the compass is a permanent part of your classroom, refer to it whenever you're discussing directions.

CLEVELL HARRIS

Puzzled About Maps
Skill: Geography

Even intermediate kids think a good puzzle is worth its weight in gold! Turn any map into a floor map by gluing it onto a large piece of poster board. Use a different color of poster board for each map to make it easy to keep puzzles separate. After the map has dried, cut it into interesting shapes and store it in a labeled shoebox. Make map puzzles of any region you cover in social studies or of the settings of books the class is reading. Recruit parent volunteers to help you make these puzzles, which are perfect do-at-home projects!

Location, Location, Location!
Skill: Cardinal and intermediate directions

Give students practice in giving directions by playing Location. Choose a small but distinctive object in the classroom, such as a special eraser or figurine. Have your students close their eyes while one student places the object in a secret, but visible, location. Have students take turns asking directional questions to try to determine the object's location. For example:

- Is the object located in the northern part of the classroom?
- Is it southeast of the teacher's desk?
- Is the object located west of the aquarium?
- Is it near the northwestern corner of the classroom?

Let the first student to locate the object hide it for the next round.

Put Us on the Map!
Skill: Examining details on a map

Encourage students to dig into *every* detail of a regional map with this nifty investigation. Divide students into pairs and give each pair a copy of the reproducible on page 81. Also provide each pair with a map of the region you're planning to study. Go over the directions on the page with the class. Allow plenty of time for students to complete the activity; then have them share their findings with their classmates.

Pirate Ship
Skill: Using coordinates and directions

All aboard for this kid-pleasin' game which offers a few surprises for its sailors! Divide students into pairs. Provide each pair with four copies of page 82 and a die. (If desired, laminate one copy of the page for each player. Students can then use wipe-off markers.) Go over "To prepare to play" with students. Then discuss each step for playing the game. Be forewarned: the winner of Pirate Ship may not feel like such a winner after all!

Pizza With a World View
Skill: Culminating activity

Celebrate the completion of your mapping unit by having students create delicious Hemisphere Pizzas. First, choose a date; then check with your cafeteria manager to see if you can use the ovens that day. Next, ask parent volunteers to donate ready-made pizza crusts, pizza sauce, cheese, olives, onions, peppers, pepperoni, and other pizza fixings—enough for four large pizzas.

On pizza-making day, divide your class into four groups. Assign a hemisphere (northern, southern, eastern, and western) to each group. Have students thoroughly wash their hands, and provide them with food-handlers' gloves. Then give each group a ready-made pizza crust, fixings, and a globe or map. Instruct each group to design a pizza that looks like its assigned hemisphere. While the pizzas are cooking, review the skills students learned during the unit. Then reward them with a world-class pizza party!

Welcome to Rectanguland!

Welcome to Rectanguland! It's a nice place to visit…if you can find it! And that's where your help is needed. Follow the directions below to make an accurate map of Rectanguland. Tourists all over the world are counting on you!

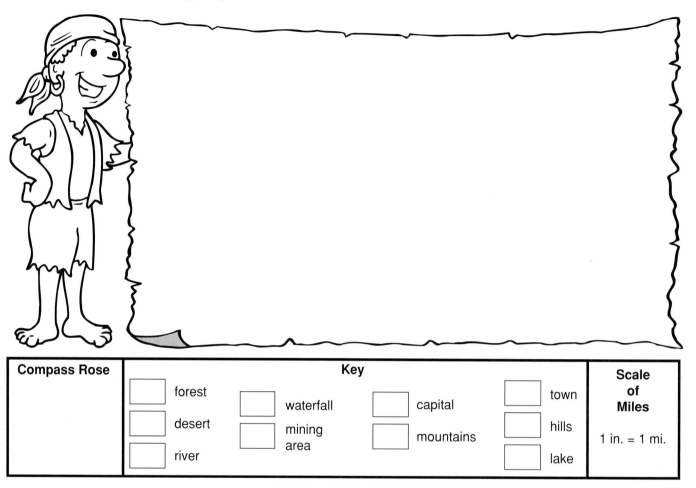

Compass Rose	**Key**			**Scale of Miles**
	☐ forest ☐ waterfall	☐ capital	☐ town	1 in. = 1 mi.
	☐ desert ☐ mining area	☐ mountains	☐ hills	
	☐ river		☐ lake	

Directions:

1. Look at each feature listed in the key. Draw and color a symbol for each feature in the box beside it.
2. Draw the compass rose. Include both cardinal and intermediate directions.
3. Now follow the steps below to make your map in the space above. Include each feature and its name.
   a. Rectanguland is a country shaped like a rectangle. (Surprised?) Its northern and southern borders are longer than its eastern and western borders.
   b. The Angular Mountains are located along the northern border.
   c. Winsome River flows down from the mountains in a southeasterly direction. Then it flows through Hiccup Hills.
   d. Winsome River forms Cascade Falls as it empties into Lake Linger. Lake Linger is near the eastern border.
   e. The capital city, Rightanglia, is located on the central western border of Rectanguland.
   f. The Great Piney Forest is also along the western border.
   g. The town of Needling is located at the northeast edge of the forest.
   h. Two miles south of Needling is its twin town of Noodling.
   i. In the south central area of the country is the DooWaka Desert.
   j. The mining center, with the town of Nugget at its center, is north of the desert.

> **Bonus Box:** Find the area of Rectanguland. Round the length of each border to the nearest half-inch.

©The Mailbox® • *Social Studies* • TEC60939 • Key p. 112

80   **Note to the teacher:** Use with "Welcome to Rectanguland!" on page 77.

Names _____

Investigating a map

SCORE:

Put Us on the Map!

Directions for partners:

1. Each player writes his or her initials in the "letters" column, one letter per box.
2. With your partner, decide on a Bonus Category and write it at the top of the last column.
3. Explore your map together to find names of places that begin with the letters of your initials.
4. Score five points for each discovery! **Hint:** Words in columns 1, 2, and 4 should be proper names, like *Alabama (A)*, *Hudson Bay (H)*, and *New York City (N)*. Words in column 3 should be common nouns, like *mountain (M)*, *valley (V)*, *boundary (B)*, *state (S)*, etc.
5. Total up your score and write it on the map above.

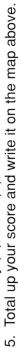

letters (initials)	① political areas (countries, states)	② bodies of water (lakes, rivers)	③ landforms (mountain, valley, etc.)	④ cities and towns	⑤ Bonus Category
Player 1					
Player 2					

©The Mailbox® • *Social Studies* • TEC60939

Note to the teacher: Use with "Put Us on the Map!" on page 79. Help students who may have difficulty selecting a Bonus Category by listing suggestions such as these on the board: Specific Mountain Ranges/Peaks, Airports, Counties, Historic Landmarks, National/State Parks, Colleges and Universities.

Pirate Ship

To prepare to play:

1. Stand a book or two between you and your opponent so that you can't see each other's grids. Turn one copy of the grid over.
2. Name five prizes you would like to win. Your opponent writes each prize in a different oval on one of his or her grids. Your opponent then names five prizes he or she wants to win. Write each one in a different oval on one of your grids.
3. Next, your opponent writes five dud prizes for you (rusty nails, rotten sneaker, etc.) in five different ovals on his or her grid. Write five dud prizes for your opponent on your grid.
4. Place your two grids beside each other. You will record your moves on the blank grid. You will record your opponent's moves on the prize grid.

The goal is to be the first player to find five prizes. To earn a prize, you must call out all the coordinate pairs that are enclosed by a prize oval. Remember: some prize ovals only have two coordinate pairs, while others have three.

To play:

1. Player 1 calls out a pair of coordinates, such as (D, 4). He marks the location with a small X on his blank grid.
2. Player 2 finds those coordinates and marks them with a small X on her prize grid. If the X falls inside one of the prize ovals, Player 2 says "hit." If the X doesn't fall inside a prize oval, Player 2 says "miss."
3. Player 1 then rolls the die. He may move one block at a time according to the roll of the die. For example, if a three is rolled, Player 1 might say, "Move one block north from (D, 4), one block east, and another block east." Player 1 would now be at (F, 5). Player 2 marks the location of those coordinates on her prize grid with a small X and says "hit" or "miss". Player 1 also marks this coordinate pair on his blank grid.
4. Player 2 then takes a turn, calling out a pair of coordinates and then rolling the die.
5. When Player 1 takes his next turn, he can start with any pair of coordinates, not just his last pair.
6. When a player has earned a prize, the opponent says "Prize earned" but does *not* reveal the name of the prize.
7. Play continues until one player wins any five prizes. That's right—*any* five prizes!

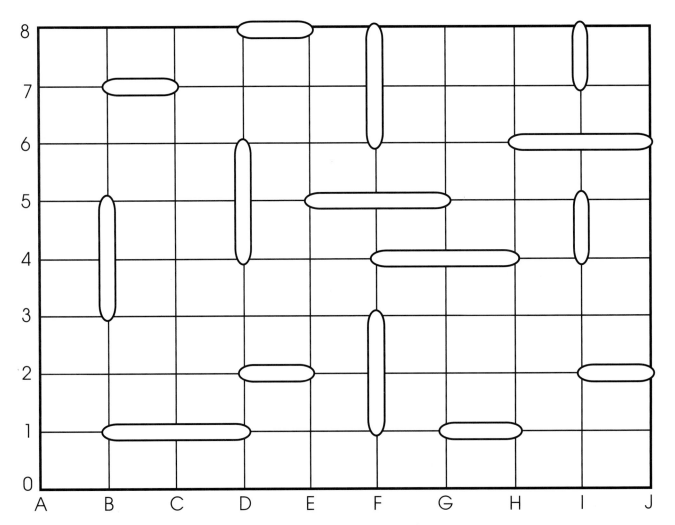

Social Studies Specials

STRIKING SOCIAL STUDIES GOLD!

Need a nifty idea to add some shine to your social studies lessons? Then dig right into this gold mine of skill-strengthening activities!

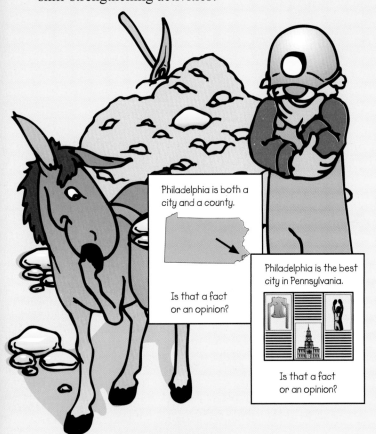

Philadelphia is both a city and a county.

Is that a fact or an opinion?

Philadelphia is the best city in Pennsylvania.

Is that a fact or an opinion?

Picture-Perfect Postcards
Skill: Research, writing

Assess what students have learned about a state, region, province, or foreign country with these supersize postcards! Tell students that each of them has just won an all-expenses-paid vacation to a foreign country. Assign each student a place; then guide him through the steps below to complete the project. To vary the activity, have the student write a note that's persuasive instead of friendly.

Materials for each student:

access to reference materials	stapler
8½" x 11" sheet of white paper	glue
12" x 18" sheet of white construction paper	crayons, colored pencils, or markers
2" square of white paper	pinking shears

Steps:

1. Research five to ten facts about your place, including information about its geography, history, climate, etc.
2. Use the facts to write an interesting note to someone you know.
3. Edit your note; then copy it onto the 8½" x 11" sheet of white paper.
4. Staple the note onto the left half of the white construction paper.
5. Write the person's name and address on the right half of the postcard.
6. Use pinking shears to trim the edges of the paper square to resemble a stamp. On it, draw a picture—such as a flag, flower, plant, or animal—to represent your place. Also write the monetary unit of your place on the stamp.
7. Glue the stamp to the upper right corner of your postcard.
8. On the other side of the postcard, draw and color a scene that illustrates your place.

Sherry Ostroff, Burrowes Elementary, Lancaster, PA

Is That a Fact?
Skill: Research, recognizing facts and opinions

Use this fun activity to help students distinguish facts from opinions while studying any social studies topic. Pair students; then give each pair colored pencils or markers and two 8½" x 11" sheets of white paper. Assign each pair a different topic from the unit being studied. Then direct the pair to research one fact on its topic and write a factual sentence about it at the top of one sheet of paper. Also have them draw a picture below this sentence to illustrate it and then write "Is that a fact or an opinion?" at the bottom of the sheet. Tell the pair to do the same with the second sheet of paper, but to write an opinion instead of a fact. When students are finished, collect the sheets, mix them up, and bind them into a class book with a title page. Share the book with the class, asking students to indicate whether each statement is a fact or an opinion, and why. It's a fact—this activity is a winner!

Lori Sammartino
Cranberry Township, PA

84

Triarama Timeline

Skill: Sequencing historical events

Enhance the study of any historical period with this eye-catching, three-dimensional timeline! On the board, list the important events of the period you are studying. Assign each student a different event. Then give him scissors, glue, crayons or markers, construction paper scraps, tape, and a copy of the triarama pattern on page 86. Have him complete the triarama as directed to illustrate his assigned event. Also have him write a paragraph about his event and tape it to his triarama as shown. Then have students pin the triaramas in the correct sequence on a bulletin board, along with a title and the date and name of each event. Be prepared—students will want to "tri" this activity again and again and again!

Kimberly Feldman
Salt Brook Elementary
New Providence, NJ

Mystery Regions

Skill: Reviewing U.S. regions

Review United States regions in style with this activity that results in some rather unique student newscasts! Divide students into groups, with one group per region. Have group members write clues about their region (without mentioning its name) to use in a news broadcast. Have one student in each group act as the anchorperson, another as a meteorologist reporting about the region's weather, and the others as reporters giving clues about the region. If desired, allow students to include clues in songs and commercials between segments of their newscast. Give students time to practice.

On the day of the broadcasts, list the regions on the board for each student to copy on his paper. As each group performs, have each member of the audience listen to the clues and identify the region being described by writing the name of the group's anchorperson next to that region on his paper. After all the presentations have been made, have each anchorperson reveal his group's region so students can check their papers.

Kathy Moses, Pocono Elementary Center, Tannersville, PA

Time Weavers

Skill: Sequence, cause and effect

Have students understand how historic events could have shaped the lives of important people with this unique timeline activity. Assign each student a different important person from the time period or area you are studying. Have the student research significant dates in that individual's life and at least four major world events that could have impacted the person in some way. After the research has been done, review with students how a timeline is constructed. Then give each student the materials listed and a copy of page 87. Guide him through the steps shown to create his own time weaver.

Materials for each student:
3" x 18" strip of white paper (or
    adding machine tape)
12" x 18" sheet of construction paper
four 1" x 8" strips of white paper
ruler
scissors
glue
pen
crayons or markers

Terry Healy
Eugene Field Elementary, Manhattan, KS

Triarama Pattern

Use with "Triarama Timeline" on page 85.

Directions

1. Cut out the square below.
2. Bring A/C to E by folding the square in half along the solid line to form a triangle. Fold it in half again along the dotted line to make a smaller triangle.
3. Unfold the square and cut along the dotted line.
4. Turn the square so that E is pointing straight up and the cut line is pointing downward. Use crayons or markers to draw the background for your scene on the large triangle above the solid line.
5. Bring C over to B and glue in place.
6. Glue A to D.
7. Use construction paper scraps to make stand-up parts for your scene. Glue the parts to the triarama's base.

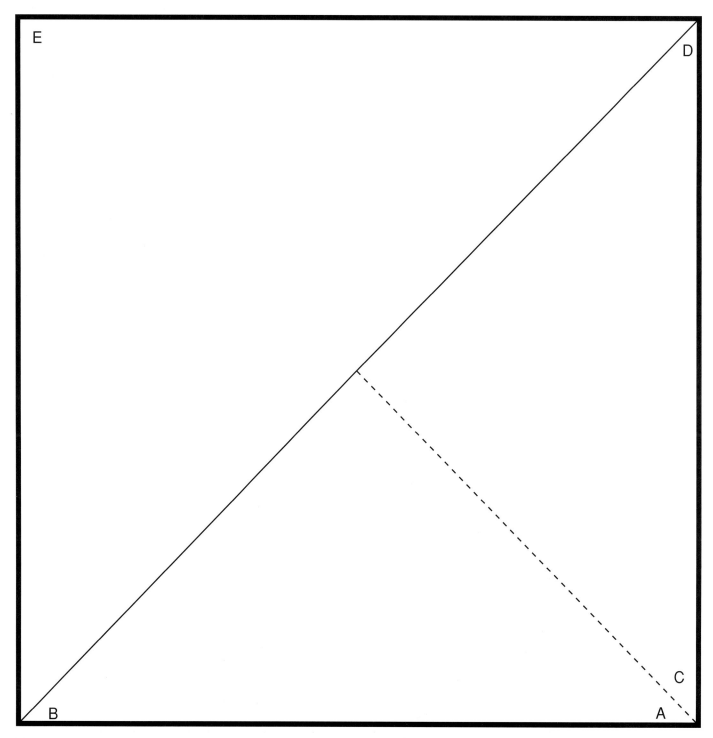

Time Weaver

Steps:

1. Measure and make cuts in the construction paper where shown by the dotted lines.
2. Beginning at one end, weave the 3" x 18" strip through the construction paper so that the ¼-inch-wide cuts hold the strip in place.
3. Write the timeline for your person's life vertically on this strip, beginning with his birth and ending with his death.
4. On the right end of each 1" x 8" strip, write a different world event and the year(s) it occurred.
5. Weave each strip under the timeline so that the writing is above the timeline and near a corresponding year in the individual's life. Glue the top and bottom of each strip to the construction paper to hold it in place.
6. Think of the effect that each world event had or could have had on your famous person. Write that effect on the bottom of each strip.
7. Title your timeline and illustrate its important events with crayons or markers.

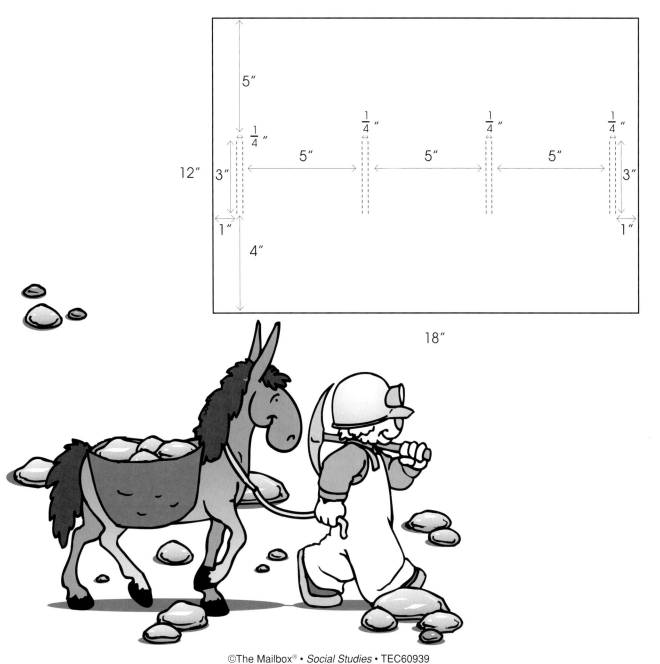

Note to the teacher: Use with "Time Weavers" on page 85.

Right on the Money!

Helping Students Understand Basic Economics

Supply and demand, goods and services, wants and needs—when's the best time to teach kids basic economics? Anytime…and all the time! Check out the following fresh and fun ideas for creating a classroom of in-the-know consumers.

by Therese Durhman

The Basics:
- No one can have everything he wants.
- Everyone must make *choices.*
- *Good choices* are based on comparing the *costs and benefits* of different *goods and services.*
- To make wise choices, one must understand the *effects of those choices.*
- Our choices create the *demand* for goods and services.
- This demand affects the *supply,* which is the *amount of goods and services* that are for sale.

Welcome to Your Dream Classroom!

Concept: Making choices

It's the ultimate classroom, where every want is fulfilled and every need is met. A dream? Yep! Illustrate the basic economic concept of making choices with this nifty introductory activity. Tell students that they're moving to a new, empty classroom, and you need their help furnishing it. Next, brainstorm and list on the board classroom needs (students' and teacher's desks, computer and printer, maps, globes, trash can, pencil sharpener, television, VCR, etc.). Then divide students into groups of four and provide each group with a catalog. Have each group develop a list of about 12 wants for the classroom (for example, video games, toys, CD player, CDs, sports equipment, etc.), plus each one's cost. While students work on their "wants" lists, write an estimated cost beside each "needs" item on the board.

When each group has completed its wants list, tell the class how much money has been budgeted for the new classroom. Make sure the amount is not much greater than the total cost of all of the needs listed on the chalkboard. Then have each group list the items it would order to furnish the new classroom, based on the budget. Ask a recorder in each group to list reasons why the group chose the items that it did. After each group shares its list of items and their total cost, have the class decide which group created the most realistic order.

You Can't Always Get What You Want

Concept: Supply and demand

Introduce setting priorities and the concept of supply and demand with this hands-on activity. First, pass around the classroom a container of small items—such as paper squares, checkers, or game chips—in two colors only. Instruct each student to take any ten items. After every child has chosen his items, write the items' values on the board (for example: blue = $1.00 and red = $5.00). Next, display an object such as a special pencil or a candy bar. Tell students that the item is for sale, but you have only one. Then start the bidding at $1.00 and sell it to the highest bidder.

After a student pays for and receives the item, display a class supply of the same item and announce that bidding for one will begin at $1.00. After students have purchased the items, ask the child who bought the first one at the high price to explain how she thinks supply and demand affected her purchase. Ask if she would have paid such a high price if she had known there were enough items for everyone to have one. Discuss why consumers often pay a high price for an object of which there is a limited supply. Then ask students to share examples of when this has happened to them in real life.

Looking for a Deal
Concept: Supply and demand

How do supply and demand affect the prices of goods? Help students understand the connection with this fun activity. First, copy the statements at the right onto a transparency or the board, omitting the answers in parentheses. Discuss the first half of each statement with students, but don't share its answer yet.

Next, instruct each student to choose three objects from her desk and write a price for each one on a sticky note. Have each child display her three objects with their accompanying price tags. Then invite students to silently circulate throughout the classroom and observe the items for sale and their prices. When students return to their desks, instruct each one to write a marketing plan based on what she observed, answering such questions as:

1. Which items are most available?
2. Which items are least available?
3. Should I choose different objects to sell? Why or why not?
4. Should I increase any of my prices? Why or why not?
5. Should I decrease any of my prices? Why or why not?

Have volunteers share their marketing strategies. Then review the statements on the transparency and ask students to supply the missing information.

If the supply of a product...
- stays the same and the demand increases, then the price will ___. *(go up)*
- stays the same and the demand decreases, then the price will ___. *(go down)*
- decreases and the demand stays the same, then the price will ___. *(go up)*
- increases and the demand stays the same, then the price will ___. *(go down)*

Supply and Demand, Cause and Effect
Concept: How supply and demand affect the market

How do supply and demand affect the market? Have students apply what they have learned in the previous activities to find out. Write each imaginary headline below on the board. Then read aloud each item below the headline. Ask students what effect they think the headline event will have on each item by responding with either a thumbs-up (increase) or a thumbs-down (decrease) gesture.

Next, have students work in small groups to brainstorm other imaginary headlines and four or five effects of each event. Have groups share their headlines and effects with the class, asking classmates to respond with thumbs-up or thumbs-down gestures.

"Sugar Crop Destroyed"
- the price of candy *(thumbs-up/increase)*
- the supply of candy *(thumbs-down/decrease)*
- the price of jelly *(thumbs-up/increase)*

"Freeze Hurts Florida Crops"
- the price of oranges *(thumbs-up/increase)*
- the supply of oranges *(thumbs-down/decrease)*
- the price of apples *(thumbs-up/increase)*

"Middle East Conflict Stops Oil Flow"
- the supply of oil *(thumbs-down/decrease)*
- the price of oil *(thumbs-up/increase)*
- the sale of large cars *(thumbs-down/decrease)*
- the price of wood-burning stoves *(thumbs-up/increase)*

To Trade or Not to Trade
Concept: Bartering

To trade or not to trade—that is the question! Introduce the concept of bartering by asking students, "How does an apple grower pay for the gasoline he uses: with money or with the apples he grows?" and, "How does the gas station owner pay his employees: with money or with gasoline?" Explain to students that in the United States, we exchange money for goods and services instead of exchanging goods and services for other goods and services. Use the following activity to help students understand why it's easier to use money as a standard of value than to use different amounts of goods or services.

First, have each student either bring an inexpensive item to class that he would like to trade with a classmate or write on an index card a service he will perform, such as carrying a classmate's books to the bus or helping with homework. Next, have students walk around the room to see what goods and services are for sale. Instruct each student to find something he'd like and trade for it. Students may make more than one trade. After trading, have each student write a brief paragraph describing the experience. Have students think about and answer in their paragraphs the questions shown.

- What money value would you give your item or service?
- What money value would you give the item or service you traded for?
- Do you feel your item or service was equal in value to what you traded for? Why or why not?
- Did you trade for what you really wanted?
- Do you feel the trade was fair? Why or why not?
- How is the value of a service determined?
- How is the value of an item determined?
- What are the advantages and disadvantages of trading?
- What are the advantages and disadvantages of having assigned money values for goods and services?

Parents with children living with them

Market Influence
Concept: Wants and needs for different age groups

How do the wants and needs of consumers help control the market? Explain to students that every time a consumer buys an item, he's "voting" to have that item produced. Producers of goods watch carefully to see what people choose. They want to know what consumers want, so that they will know which goods to produce. After deciding what to produce, the producer must decide how many of the item to make.

To help students better understand these economic issues, divide the class into four teams. Assign each team an age group to interview, such as nine to 12-year-olds, teenagers, parents with children living with them, and grandparents. Have each team survey about ten to 12 people to find out the goods and services that folks in its group buy. Suggest the following categories for the survey: entertainment, hobbies, clothes, household items, and travel. After students complete the surveys, provide each team with magazines, catalogs, and a sheet of poster board. Have the team cut out (or draw) pictures to represent the wants and needs of its interviewees. Display the posters on a bulletin board to show the differences in the wants and needs of different groups of consumers.

The Price Is...Different!
Concept: Comparing prices in different areas

Why do prices of the same item vary in different parts of the country? Examine this issue with the following research activity. With the class, list on the board five or six common grocery items that could be purchased anywhere in the country, such as Campbell's Chicken Noodle Soup, Pepsi soda, Lucky Charms cereal, oranges, ground beef, etc. Have students estimate the cost of each item if purchased in your area. After students check the prices of the items in several local stores for homework, have them calculate the average cost of each item. Display that information on a class chart as shown. If students have pen pals or relatives who live in other areas of the country, have them contact these friends to find out the prices of the exact same items in their hometowns. Or contact friends or relatives of yours who live in other geographic areas to obtain the prices. Add this information to the class chart.

Next, divide the class into groups. Have each group choose at least two locations from the chart. Then have each group compare the locations' prices and write a paragraph explaining reasons for the differences in price. After each group shares its paragraph, discuss factors that contribute to these differences in price, such as the distance from the producer to the seller, available resources in the area, and supply and demand. To complete the activity, have each student compare all of the items that you researched in a double-bar graph (with bars representing two different locations).

Item	Avg. price here	Other Geographic Areas			
		NY	FL	OH	KS
Campbell's Chicken Noodle Soup					
Pepsi soda (2-liter bottle)					
Lucky Charms Cereal					
Oranges (1-lb. bag)					
Ground Beef (1 lb.)					

Lifelong Decisions
Skill: Making economic choices

With *so much* money to spend and *so much* to choose from, kids probably think it's fun for adults to fill grown-up wants and needs! Help students understand that adults, as well as young people, must make economic choices every day because they can't have everything they want or need. Duplicate the survey on page 92 for each student. Have each student choose three adults she would like to interview, with one of the adults being the student's parent or caregiver. When the surveys are completed, have students share the responses and their written summaries in small groups. Ask students to share with the entire class some examples of choices that adults have to make; then discuss the trade-offs that are involved in making those decisions.

Making Lifelong Decisions

When you become an adult, you can have everything you want and need, right? Find out by talking to some adults that you know!

Directions:

1. Interview at least three adults to find out what kind of economic decisions they made when they were your age, as well as what kind of decisions they have to make today.
2. One of the adults should be your mom, dad, or caregiver.
3. Use the chart below to record each adult's answers to your questions.
4. Write additional notes on the back of this sheet or tape-record your interview.

	Adult #1	Adult #2	Adult #3
1. When you were my age, did you earn money? How?			
2. Did your parents give you an allowance? If so, how much and how frequently?			
3. What did you buy with your money?			
4. Did you save some of your money?			
5. Did you ever set goals for how you would use the money you earned?			
6. Did you have to make choices about how you spent your money? If so, what were some choices you had to make?			
7. Give some examples of "wants versus needs" choices you must now make as an adult.			
8. Give an example of a recent decision you have had to make about how you spend your money. What were some of the trade-offs that you had to consider?			

Summary: On another sheet of paper, write a summary of what you learned from the three adults that you interviewed.

EXTRA! EXTRA!

Social Studies Sentinel

Make your social studies lesson plans big news with this trio of hot-off-the-press activities!

Archaeological Assumptions

Try this critical-thinking exercise when studying ancient history or any historical period. Explain to students that an archaeologist must make assumptions about many of the artifacts she finds. To demonstrate, place several items, including one that students cannot immediately identify, on a tray (for example, a plastic earplug, a pen, two coins, a mirror, a comb, and a shoelace). Explain that the police have found a gym bag on school grounds. It contains no identification, so the police want students' help in learning more about the possible owner of the bag. Display the items as the bag's contents. After examining the items, have each group write a descriptive profile of the bag's owner to share with the class. When the groups make somewhat different assumptions based on the same evidence (and they will!), help students conclude that personal and cultural experiences can impact their assumptions. End by discussing how this can make an archaeologist's job a challenge.
Dr. Donna M. McDougall, Kearny, AZ

Story Map Review

Conclude a unit on any state, region, country, or historical period with this headline-grabbing activity! For each group, use an opaque projector to draw an outline map of the state, region, or country being studied. Have each group illustrate its map to show the major topics covered during the unit. Challenge students to position their illustrations in the areas to which they pertain. For example, to review the pre–Civil War period, the Northeast could be illustrated with factories and various products, the Southeast with plantations and cotton fields, the Midwest with pioneers moving west on Conestoga wagons, and the West with miners panning for gold. As groups share their maps with the class, you can quickly assess what students know!

What State Am I?

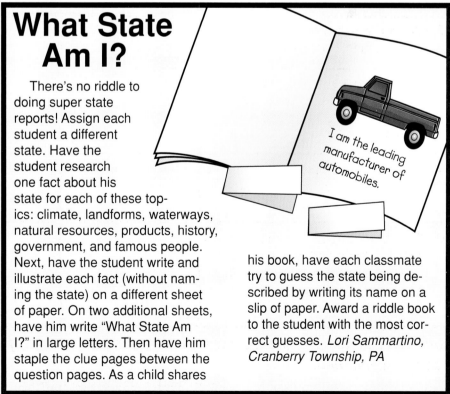

I am the leading manufacturer of automobiles.

There's no riddle to doing super state reports! Assign each student a different state. Have the student research one fact about his state for each of these topics: climate, landforms, waterways, natural resources, products, history, government, and famous people. Next, have the student write and illustrate each fact (without naming the state) on a different sheet of paper. On two additional sheets, have him write "What State Am I?" in large letters. Then have him staple the clue pages between the question pages. As a child shares his book, have each classmate try to guess the state being described by writing its name on a slip of paper. Award a riddle book to the student with the most correct guesses. *Lori Sammartino, Cranberry Township, PA*

Celebrate Citizenship!

Activities on the Rights and Responsibilities of Citizenship

Salute citizenship—with all of its rights and responsibilities—using the following creative activities and reproducibles!

with ideas by Pat Twohey, Old County Road School, Smithfield, RI

Vocabulary Explosion
Concept: Terms related to citizenship

Create a dazzling fireworks display with this star-spangled vocabulary activity! After dividing the class into pairs, give each twosome a marker and a fireworks shape cut from red, white, or blue construction paper. Assign a term listed below to each pair; then have the twosome label the cutout with its word. Next, direct the partners to research the word and write its definition on the back of the cutout. After each pair shares its term, hang the fireworks from your ceiling with string. If desired, have each student record the terms and meanings in his own word journal. Have students make their journals using these steps:

1. Place eight sheets of white paper between two sheets of construction paper (one red, one blue).
2. Staple the white paper between the covers at the top.
3. Trim the journal to make a fireworks shape as shown.
4. Write each word and its definition in the journal, one word per page. Add an illustration that symbolizes or helps explain the word.
5. Label the journal "[Your name]'s Liberty Lexicon" and decorate the cover.

We, the Citizens
Concept: Meaning of citizenship

Encourage students to reflect on what it means to be a citizen with this poetry-writing activity. In advance, collect an empty coffee can (with the lid) for each student. List these questions on the board:

- What does it mean to be a citizen?
- What rights does a citizen enjoy?
- What responsibilities or duties does a citizen have?
- Why be a member of a nation instead of acting on your own?

Divide the class into groups to discuss the questions. Then have students share their ideas as you list them on chart paper. Guide students through the list shown below, pointing out that many rights have limits. For example, the freedom of speech doesn't allow a person to harm another person's reputation by telling lies.

Next, give each student a lidded coffee can. Have each student measure and cut a piece of white construction paper to fit around the can. Have the student write a poem on the paper about what citizenship means to her. After the student illustrates the poem, have her glue the paper around the can. Challenge each group formed earlier to come up with a unique way to display the decorated cans; then vote to select the class's favorite idea. Invite other classes to view your students' salute to citizenship.

Terms
alien
Bill of Rights
citizen
civil rights
Constitution
duty
freedom of assembly
freedom of religion
freedom of speech
national
nationality
naturalization
right
taxes
visa
vote

Rights of U.S. citizens include the following:

- freedom of speech
- freedom of religion
- freedom of assembly
- right to vote
- right to run for political offices
- right to travel throughout the United States
- can't be forced to leave homeland
- can't lose citizenship except for serious actions

Celebrating Citizenship

by Shellie

Name That Right!
Concept: Rights of citizenship

Use this nifty game to help students focus on the ways citizens exercise their rights every day. Divide the class into groups. Give each group three four-inch paper squares: one red, one white, and one blue. Write the following code on the board: red = freedom of speech, blue = freedom of religion, white = freedom of assembly. Have each group discuss these rights; then have it write on each card two situations during which a citizen would exercise that right (for example, a group might list "moving to a new town and deciding which church to attend" on the blue card). Give each group a folder in which to store its completed cards. Then play the following guessing game:

1. In turn, have one student from Group A read aloud a situation from one of his group's cards, keeping the card hidden in the folder.
2. Challenge Group B to identify the right that matches the situation.
3. Have Group A display the card that was read. If the guess is correct, award a red chip, plastic checker, or paper marker to Group B.
4. Repeat Steps 1–3 with Group B reading a situation to Group C. Continue until all situations on the cards have been read and discussed. Then declare the team with the most chips the winner.

moving to a new town and deciding which church to attend

worshipping at a local synagogue

an environmentalist giving a speech on stopping pollution

a politician giving a campaign speech

holding a march to protest a new law

attending a meeting on a proposed park

Citizens Speak Out
Concept: The Bill of Rights

Introduce your class to the most famous Bill around. Bill Gates? No! The Bill of Rights, of course! Give each student a copy of page 97, a kid-friendly version of this famous document. Divide the class into pairs; then have each twosome read through the ten amendments and discuss what they think each one means and why it is important. Have the pair list on the back of the page three main ideas it gathered from reading the amendments. Then discuss the students' ideas as a class. Next, have each student complete the second part of page 97 as directed. Provide time for each child to give his speech to the class.

Serve on Juries

Pay Taxes

by Brian

Do Your Duty, by George!
Concept: Responsibilities of citizenship

If George Washington—one of our country's most famous citizens—were alive today, he'd probably have plenty to say during this activity on the duties of citizenship. Point out that most nations require each citizen to pay taxes, defend his country, and obey laws. Many of those governments also require that certain citizens serve on juries. Discuss these duties, asking students to give reasons why citizens should (or should not) fulfill them. After the discussion, provide each student with a copy of page 98, a 9" x 12" sheet of gray construction paper, scissors, glue, and clear tape. Have each student complete his monument and share it with the class; then display the projects in the classroom or school library.

Unwritten Duties

Concept: Responsibilities of citizenship

Many people believe that citizens also have duties that are not demanded by the law. Challenge students to use this data collection activity to find out what others in the community think about these unwritten responsibilities. Give each student a form similar to the one shown. Instruct each child to poll a total of ten to 15 adults (family members, neighbors, and other adult friends) and fill out his form.

After students have finished their polls, divide the class into groups of four. Give each group a sheet of chart paper, a marker, and a ruler. Direct the students in each group to combine their data and create a bar graph to display their results for each question. Then instruct each group to analyze its graph and prepare an oral presentation to explain the findings. After each group gives its presentation, discuss these questions: What do the statistics tell us? How would you have answered the questions, and why?

Citizenship Poll

Do you agree that it is a citizen's duty to...	Yes	No
Vote	卌 卌 |||	||
Learn about public problems	卌 卌		||||
Help other people in the community	卌 卌 |||	||

Reading About Citizenship

Concept: Making connections to citizenship

Help students make connections to the topic of citizenship with the aid of children's books. Ask your librarian to help you gather copies of titles about citizenship. Display the questions shown below. Then read one of the books aloud and use the questions to guide a class discussion. After the talk, divide the class into groups. Give each group one or more books, a sheet of chart paper, and a marker. Have the group list its responses to the questions on the paper. Then have groups share their responses as a class.

Discussion questions:

- How is this story related to the topic of citizenship?
- What question(s) does this story raise for you?
- What is your opinion of this story?

Speaking of Your Rights

What's the most famous Bill in the United States? The Bill of Rights, of course! This document states the first ten amendments to the U.S. Constitution. These amendments guarantee the basic freedoms that Americans—including you—enjoy today!

Part I: Read through the summary of the Bill of Rights below. Talk with your partner about what you think each amendment means and why it is important.

Amendment 1
You have freedoms of religion, speech, and the press. You also have the right to assemble peacefully and to let the government know if you disagree with its actions.

Amendment 2
You have the right to own and bear arms (weapons).

Amendment 3
Soldiers won't be kept in your home during peaceful times without your permission.

Amendment 4
You or your property cannot be searched or taken without your permission or without a warrant based on a good reason.

Amendment 5
You can't be held for a crime without an indictment from a grand jury (except in some military cases). You can't be tried twice for the same crime. You don't have to testify against yourself in court. You have the right to due process of the law. Your property can't be taken for public use without payment.

Amendment 6
You have the right to a speedy and public trial by a fair jury. You have the right to know what you're accused of and to hear any witnesses against you. You have the right to find witnesses to support you and to have a lawyer defend you.

Amendment 7
You have the right to a trial by jury.

Amendment 8
You can't be charged excessive fines or bail or be punished in a cruel or unusual way.

Amendment 9
You have other rights that are not specifically listed in the Constitution.

Amendment 10
The federal government may have only the powers given to it by the Constitution. Any other powers belong to the states and to the people.

Part II: Choose one of the amendments above. On another sheet of paper, write a short speech giving your opinion of the amendment. Tell why you think it is or is not an important right for citizens to have and what life might be like without it. Practice your speech so you'll be ready to present it to the rest of the class.

©The Mailbox® • Social Studies • TEC60939

Do Your Duty, by George!

The Washington Monument in Washington, DC, honors one of our country's most famous citizens—George Washington. Make George proud by making your own mini monument about citizenship.

On each side of the pattern, list at least two reasons why citizens should carry out each duty. Then cut out the pattern and glue it to a sheet of construction paper. Cut out the pattern again and fold it on the dotted lines. Then tape the sides together to create your monument (see the illustration).

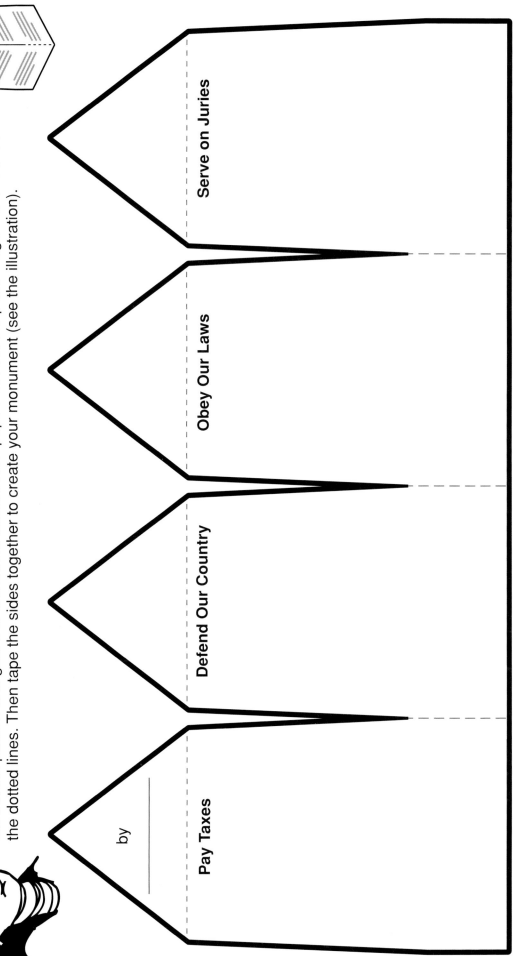

by _____

Pay Taxes

Defend Our Country

Obey Our Laws

Serve on Juries

98

Note to the teacher: Use with "Do Your Duty, by George!" on page 95. Provide each student with scissors, glue, a 9" x 12" sheet of gray construction paper, and clear tape.

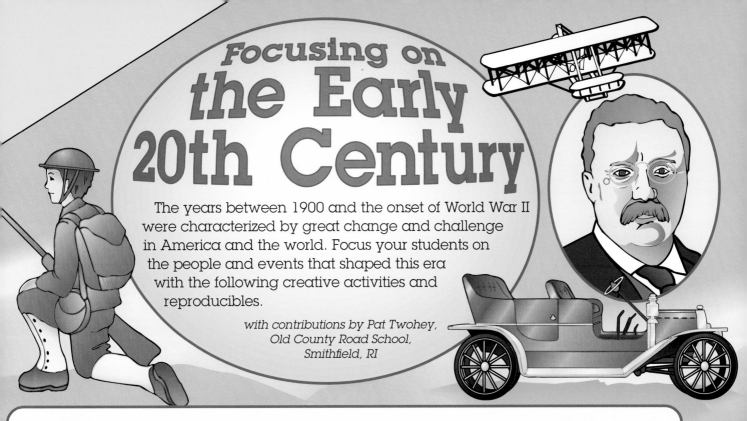

Focusing on the Early 20th Century

The years between 1900 and the onset of World War II were characterized by great change and challenge in America and the world. Focus your students on the people and events that shaped this era with the following creative activities and reproducibles.

with contributions by Pat Twohey, Old County Road School, Smithfield, RI

World War I: Causes and Results

Skills: Classifying, using context clues

Help your students understand the major causes and results of the Great War, or World War I (1914–1918), with this activity. Divide the class into groups of three or four students each. Give each group a copy of page 102, scissors, a glue stick, and a 12" x 18" sheet of construction paper. Inform students that they are going to be learning about World War I. Then challenge them to complete page 102 as directed, using context clues to help them arrange (but not glue) the strips on the construction paper. When students are finished, check and discuss their charts using the answer key on page 112. Allow a group to rearrange any incorrectly placed strips before it glues them to the paper. After students have studied World War I, have groups, pairs, or individual students repeat the activity on page 102 as a quick review or assessment.

Causes of World War I	Reasons USA Entered War	Results of World War I

Headlines

- Jim Thorpe Loses Olympic Medals
- Lindbergh Flies Across Atlantic
- Peary Reaches North Pole
- Typhoid Mary Imprisoned
- Earthquake Devastates San Francisco
- President McKinley Shot
- Wright Brothers Make Powered Flight
- Queen Victoria of England Dies
- Marie Curie Wins Nobel Prize
- Prohibition Begins Today
- *Titanic* Sinks on Maiden Voyage
- King Tut's Tomb Found
- Henry Ford Unveils First Assembly Line
- *Lusitania* Sunk by Germans
- Tsar Nicholas Steps Down
- Pancho Villa Raids American Towns

Breaking News: Big Stories of the Era

Skills: Writing a news report, researching a topic

One thing's for sure—there was a lot of news to report during the early years of the 20th century! Introduce students to some of these news stories with this partner activity. Ask your school's librarian to provide your class with resources on early 20th-century America. Write each headline listed on a strip of paper; then place the strips in a bag. Next, divide the class into pairs. Have each twosome pull a strip from the bag, research the event, and write a brief television news report that answers who, what, where, when, why, and how. Each day during your unit, ask one or two twosomes to share their breaking news reports. For fun, decorate a bulletin board with a globe cutout and the title "World News Today." Position two student desks in front of the display; then have the reporting students don old suit jackets and ties and sit at the desks to give their report.

Women and the Vote
Skills: Expressive and persuasive writing

On an August day in 1920, a decades-long struggle ended when the 19th Amendment was signed into law. American women finally had the right to vote. To focus students on this historic event, announce that your school is holding an election to select a new mascot. Everyone will be allowed to vote except for students in your grade level. After your students protest (and they will!), ask each child to write a paragraph about how your announcement makes him feel. Let volunteers share their paragraphs.

Next, explain that the announcement was bogus. Point out that the frustration students felt is similar to that experienced by many American women in the early 20th century. Share the information shown above; then discuss the passage of the 19th Amendment. Conclude by having each student pretend to be a suffragist and write a letter to persuade his representative to vote in favor of the 19th Amendment. In the letter, have the student explain how women's suffrage will benefit the country and why voting for the 19th Amendment is the right thing to do. If desired, let students design posters that might have been seen at a suffrage rally before the 1920 vote. Display the letters and posters on a bulletin board titled "You Vote, Girl!"

The Great Depression
Skills: Sequencing, journal writing

Examine the causes of the depression and how it affected everyday folks with this activity. After discussing the depression, give each student a copy of page 103. Have each student complete Part 1 as directed. Then divide the class into small groups. Have group members compare their answers and decide together on a final sequence. Check the groups' answers as a class and discuss how the depression affected American life. Then have each student complete Part 2. For a sharing session, group students according to the person they selected. Have students in each group read their journal entries to each other.

As a variation, have each student complete Part 2 on a six-inch paper square (leaving a margin along the left side). After the group sharing session, give each student the materials listed and display the steps shown. Place the completed booklets in your class library for students to read in their spare time.

From the Journal of Edith Miller

Materials for each student: two 6" construction paper squares, crayons or markers, scissors, glue stick, stapler, three 6" squares of writing paper, pencil

Steps:

1. Color the portrait of your person, cut it out, and glue it to a construction paper square. Add a title such as "From the Diary of [name of person]."
2. Place the pieces of writing paper behind your journal entry. Then staple the papers between the two covers to make a booklet.
3. After you study the New Deal, write another entry explaining how its programs have affected you and your life.

Who Will Make It Onto Mount Amerimore?

Americans to Research

1. Theodore Roosevelt
2. Woodrow Wilson
3. Herbert Hoover
4. Franklin Delano Roosevelt
5. Eleanor Roosevelt
6. Frank Lloyd Wright
7. Calvin Coolidge
8. Mary Pickford
9. Helen Keller
10. Walter Reed
11. George Gershwin
12. Henry Ford
13. Robert Peary
14. Babe Ruth
15. Jane Addams
16. Amelia Earhart
17. Nellie Tayloe Ross
18. Duke Ellington
19. Matthew Henson
20. Jim Thorpe
21. Charles Lindbergh
22. Langston Hughes
23. Carrie Chapman Catt
24. Robert Frost

Americans Who Made a Difference

Skills: Researching, writing and giving a speech

Early 20th-century America was filled with amazing Americans who did amazing things. Acquaint your students with just a few of these famous folks with this activity. Begin by displaying a picture of Mount Rushmore. Explain to students that the U.S. government has asked a famous sculptor to create a similar monument, called Mount Amerimore, to honor five Americans who made important contributions during the early 20th century. Assign to each student a name from the list shown. Then have the student research his person and write a speech nominating him or her to be one of the honorees featured on Mount Amerimore. Remind students to include facts in their speeches that justify the person's nomination.

After each child gives his speech to the class, distribute a ballot that lists the nominees. Then have each student vote for the five people he believes most deserve to be honored. If desired, have each student with a winning nominee lead a different team of classmates in sketching a design for the monument.

Literature Links

Skills: Taking notes, writing a book review

If you want to integrate a study of early 20th-century America with your literature groups, then there are plenty of terrific books ready to be read! Ask your librarian to provide you with a collection of fiction and nonfiction titles related to this time period (1900–1940). Have each child select a book. Then give each student a sheet of duplicating paper. Have her fold the paper into thirds and label it as shown. As the student reads, direct her to note on the bookmark any events, people, places, or actions related to early 20th-century America. Each day ask a few students to share any notes they have recently made on their bookmarks.

When a student finishes her book, have her use the bookmark to write a review of the book. Instruct the student to end the review with a summary of what she learned about the early 20th century while reading.

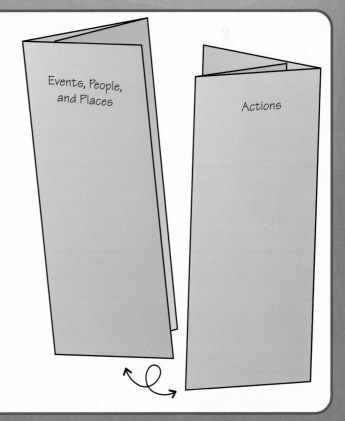

Focusing on World War I

Directions: Cut out the three boldfaced strips. Arrange them in three columns on your paper. Then cut out the other strips. Read each strip and place it in the correct column. (Hint: The numbers on the boldfaced strips tell you how many strips are in each column.)

Causes of World War I (6)	Reasons USA Entered War (2)	Results of World War I (8)
a. In Europe, people had strong feelings of pride in their own nation. Competition and angry feelings between countries grew. People in some countries wanted to rule themselves and be independent.	b. The U.S. government was angry that Germany tried to convince Mexico to go to war against the United States.	
c. Because the war cost countries so much money, nations had large debts after the war. This caused problems with the economies in these countries.	d. Because of the war, much land and property in Europe was destroyed.	
e. European nations began to compete for colonies in Africa and Asia. This created bad feelings between nations.	f. The U.S. government was angry that German submarines attacked U.S. ships.	
g. Many European countries began to build up their militaries because of greater tensions in Europe.	h. Because countries wanted to avoid another world war, a new international peacekeeping organization called the League of Nations was formed.	
i. Almost 10 million soldiers died. About 21 million more were wounded. Many other people died of disease, starvation, and other causes related to the war.	j. To keep Germany from starting another war, the size of its army and weapons supply was cut back. It was also not allowed to have submarines or aircraft.	
k. The future leader of Austria-Hungary, Archduke Francis Ferdinand, was assassinated in Bosnia-Herzegovina. Austria-Hungary then declared war on Serbia.	l. Because of the war, Germany lost some of its land to other countries.	
m. Because of the war, several old empires collapsed and new countries—such as Austria, Hungary, and Turkey—were created.	n. Because Germany was blamed for causing the war, it was punished most harshly under the Treaty of Versailles. This created some of the conditions that led to World War II about 20 years later.	
o. Alliances brought more countries into the war. For example, Russia decided to help Serbia fight Austria-Hungary. So Germany declared war on Russia. Then France (which was in an alliance with Russia) declared war on Germany.	p. Many European countries were afraid of war, so they formed alliances, or partnerships. If one country in an alliance was attacked, the other countries in the alliance agreed to help it. The Triple Entente was an alliance formed by France, Russia, and Great Britain. Germany, Austria-Hungary, and Italy formed the Triple Alliance.	

Note to the teacher: Use with "World War I: Causes and Results" on page 99.

Faces of the Great Depression

At the start of 1929, life in America looked pretty good. Unfortunately, the good times weren't to last for long. A combination of circumstances led to one of the most difficult periods in America's history. Complete the following activities about this era known as the Great Depression.

Part 1: Number these events in the order in which they occurred.

_____ People buy stock on credit to try to make more money.

_____ World War I ends.

_____ Factories increase production of goods.

_____ The Great Depression begins.

_____ Americans buy huge amounts of goods.

_____ President Franklin D. Roosevelt proposes New Deal programs to end the depression.

_____ Demand for products falls because people can't afford to keep purchasing them.

_____ Many banks and businesses fail. Many people lose their jobs.

_____ Warehouses and stores become full of products that go unsold.

_____ Stock prices drop drastically. Many investors lose all of their money.

Part 2: Pretend that it is 1932. Choose one of the people shown on this page. On another sheet of paper, write a journal entry as that person. Tell how the Great Depression has affected you. Write about your experiences, feelings, concerns, hopes, and ideas.

Edith Miller
Store Clerk

Maddie O'Brien
Factory Worker

Harry Newman
Schoolboy

E. M. Johnson
Banker

Josiah Bancroft
Farmer

Eli Warton
Store Owner

Mary Wallace
Farm Worker

Nicholas Costas
Railroad Worker

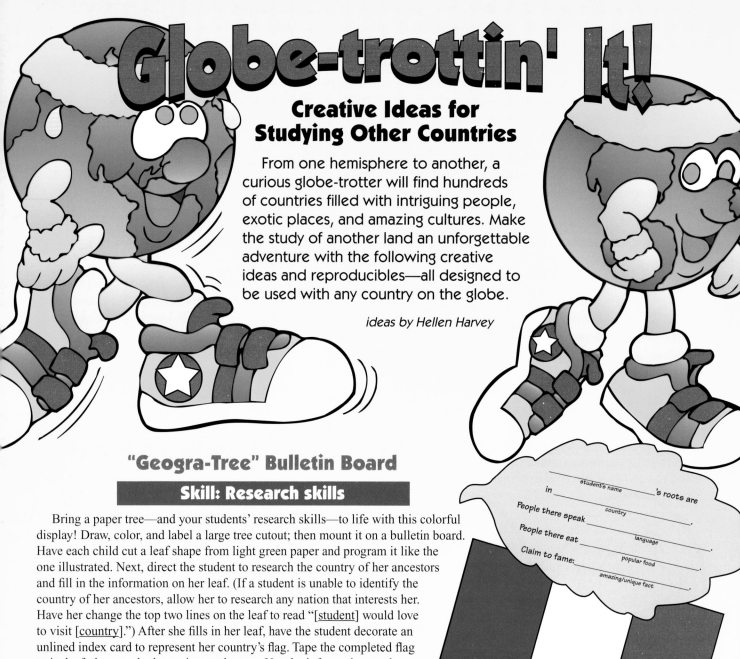

Globe-trottin' It!

Creative Ideas for Studying Other Countries

From one hemisphere to another, a curious globe-trotter will find hundreds of countries filled with intriguing people, exotic places, and amazing cultures. Make the study of another land an unforgettable adventure with the following creative ideas and reproducibles—all designed to be used with any country on the globe.

ideas by Hellen Harvey

In _____ student's name _____'s roots are
in _____ country _____.
People there speak _____ language _____.
People there eat _____ popular food _____.
Claim to fame: _____ amazing/unique fact _____.

"Geogra-Tree" Bulletin Board

Skill: Research skills

Bring a paper tree—and your students' research skills—to life with this colorful display! Draw, color, and label a large tree cutout; then mount it on a bulletin board. Have each child cut a leaf shape from light green paper and program it like the one illustrated. Next, direct the student to research the country of her ancestors and fill in the information on her leaf. (If a student is unable to identify the country of her ancestors, allow her to research any nation that interests her. Have her change the top two lines on the leaf to read "[student] would love to visit [country].") After she fills in her leaf, have the student decorate an unlined index card to represent her country's flag. Tape the completed flag to its leaf; then staple the project to the tree. Use the information on the leaves to spark many interesting discussions or as informative five-minute fillers!

Help Wanted!

Skill: Drawing conclusions, narrative writing

Have students investigate the relationships between a country's economy and the jobs available to its people with this thought-provoking activity. First, review with students what they've learned about the natural resources, climate, agriculture, and manufacturing of the country you're studying. Based on this information, what jobs might be most abundant in this land? For example, forestry and forest products provide 40% of Finland's exports, so jobs in forestry, woodworking, and paper-manufacturing industries would probably be plentiful there. Next, have each student pretend that she has found herself without money in the country you're studying. Instruct her to write a narrative in which she explains her situation, lists five jobs she applies for and her qualifications for them, and tells about the job she finally gets. After the student shares her story with the class, challenge her to explain why the job she wound up getting is likely to be available in that country.

"Geo-Bingo"

Skill: Research skills, categorizing

Whether you're studying one country or several countries at a time, this version of bingo is guaranteed to generate lots of learning! A few days before the game, list the categories shown on a sheet of chart paper. Give each student three index cards. Assign a category to each child; then have him find three facts about the country being studied that relate to his category. Direct him to write his category and one fact on each index card. Collect and shuffle the cards; then number them sequentially. When you're ready to play, follow these steps:

1. Give each student one sheet of unlined paper and a supply of paper squares to use as markers.
2. Instruct the student to fold his paper in half four times to create his game card. (When opened, the paper's folds should create a grid of 16 spaces.)
3. Have the student randomly copy one category from the chart in each space on his paper, repeating a category if he desires.
4. Read the fact from the first card. Have each student determine the fact's category.
5. If the student has the matching category on his sheet, have him cover it with a marker. Announce the number on that fact card so students who covered that category can write the number on that marker.
6. Repeat Steps 4 and 5 until a student has four markers in a row horizontally, vertically, or diagonally.
7. Check the winner's matches for correctness by having him read aloud the numbers written on his four markers. If they correctly match the numbers on the facts you've read, declare him the winner. If not, continue play.

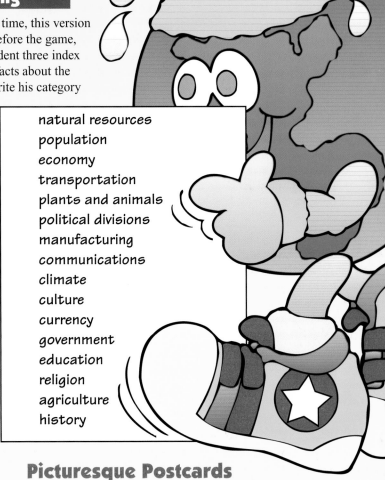

natural resources
population
economy
transportation
plants and animals
political divisions
manufacturing
communications
climate
culture
currency
government
education
religion
agriculture
history

Picturesque Postcards

Skill: Writing a description

Treat your students to this geography project worth writing home about! Give each student a 4" x 6" unlined index card, colored markers, and a 1" x ¾" piece cut from a self-sticking nametag. Assign each student a landmark from a country currently being studied. Direct the student to draw a picture of the landmark on one side of his card and address the other side like a postcard, leaving space for a note. Next, have him write the note, including a description of the landmark, its location, and its historic or geographic significance. Then, on the nametag piece, have the child design a postage stamp that's representative of that country and affix it to his postcard as a stamp. Pin these postcards on a bulletin board. With such picturesque postcards to admire, you might have to stop yourself from mailing them!

Unlikely Sports

Skill: Research skills, critical thinking

Bobsledding in Jamaica? Sounds nuts, but it's true. Share with students that despite an average temperature of 80°F, Jamaica sent a bobsled team to the Winter Games. Then divide students into groups. Have each group list the sports played in a country you're studying; then have it think about how that country's climate, topography, and culture might affect the playing of those sports. If the group thinks a sport is "unlikely" based upon one or more of the three factors, ask its members to determine what adaptations were made to make playing that sport possible. For example, even though the average temperature in Iceland is about 41°F, people there can swim year-round in heated indoor pools. Finally challenge each student to list three sports she would not expect to be played in that country and why. Provide time for students to share their lists.

Currency Conversion

Skill: Rounding decimals, multiplication

Shopping—a favorite pastime when visiting another country—can get tricky when a different currency is involved. For an exercise in converting the currency of the country you're studying, ask each student to bring in a weekly grocery-store circular. Then follow these steps:

Item	Price in U.S. dollars	Price rounded to nearest U.S. dollar	Currency per U.S. $ rounded to nearest unit	Price in foreign units
crackers	$1.98	$2.00	6 krone	12 krone

1. Have each student draw a chart as shown below on a sheet of paper.
2. Tell students to pretend they each have $10 in U.S. currency. Have each student look in his circular and list the items he'd like to buy on the chart, making sure that they don't total more than $10. Next to each item, have him list its price and that price rounded to the nearest dollar.
3. Give each student a duplicated copy of the "Currency Trading" box from a copy of *The Wall Street Journal* newspaper. This section lists exchange rates and can be found by looking in the paper's index under "Exchange Rates."
4. Explain that the "Currency per U.S. $" column tells how much of the unit from a country is equal to one U.S. dollar.
5. Write the following formula on the board: *price (rounded to nearest U.S. dollar) x currency per U.S. $ (rounded to nearest unit) = approximate price in foreign units.* With the class, use this formula to convert the rounded price of the first item to the unit of the country you're studying. Repeat with other amounts.
6. Have each student convert the price of each item on his list and fill in the rest of his chart as shown.

If students need extra practice with multiplying decimals, don't ask them to round any of the numbers. Allow students to use calculators if desired.

Global Sharing With the Peace Corps

If you'd like your students to learn firsthand about another country and its culture, then the Peace Corps' World Wise Schools program is for you! This program matches your class with a Peace Corps Volunteer serving somewhere in the world. The letters and drawings your class sends to their Peace Corps friend can include tidbits about the class's activities as well as information about your city, state, and country. In turn, the volunteer's letters can provide your class with interesting and exciting facts about his or her corner of the world.

Barbara Spilman Lawson, Waynesboro, VA

Fact-Finding Sheets

Skill: Note taking, writing paragraphs

Need a great aid to keep students from copying information when researching a country? Just give each student a copy of page 107. This sheet will guide each child's note taking by helping him recognize the important facts to research. After the student fills in the sheet's boxes with notes, have him use those notes to write a paragraph for each box. With this handy guide, be prepared to see a marked difference in both note taking *and* paragraph writing!

Mary Ann Miller, Pleasant Grove Middle School, Texarkana, TX

Fact-Finding Sheet on _____
country

★ Location in World ★	★ Capital ★	★ Money ★
★ Type of Government ★	★ Agriculture ★	★ Population and People ★
★ Head of Government ★	★ Most Important Industry ★	★ Early History ★
★ Special Foods ★	★ Recreation ★	★ Education ★
★ Famous Citizen ★	★ Flag ★	★ Official Language ★

Note to the teacher: Use with "Fact-Finding Sheets" on page 106.

All Set to Travel!

Finding out as much as you can about a place before you visit it can make the trip more pleasant and memorable. Complete the activities below to make sure your trip is nothing but fun!

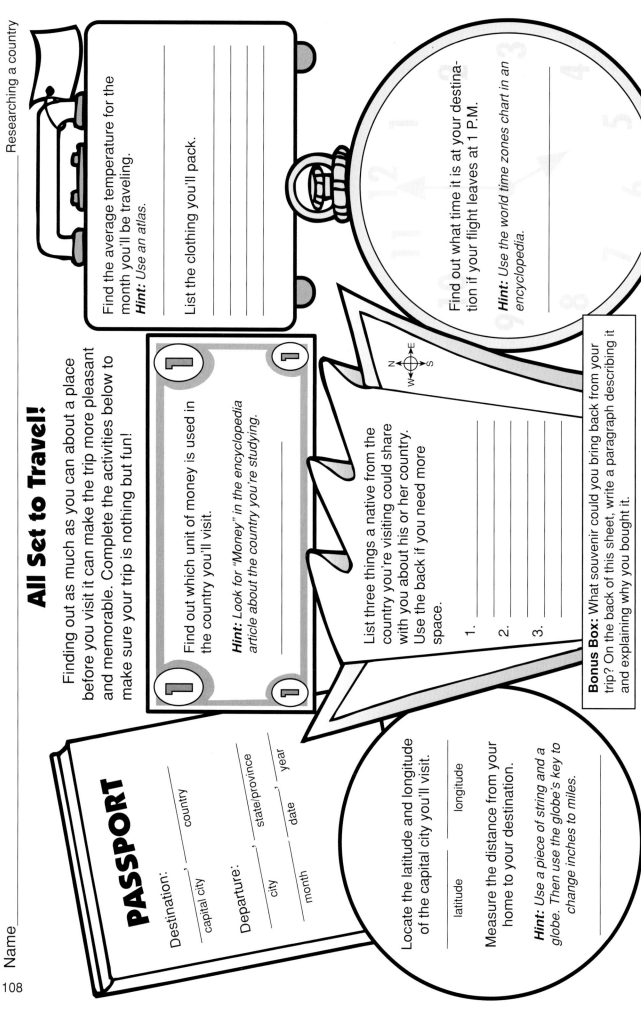

PASSPORT

Destination:
_____, _____
capital city   country

Departure:
_____, _____
city   state/province

_____, _____
month, date   year

Locate the latitude and longitude of the capital city you'll visit.

_____   _____
latitude   longitude

Measure the distance from your home to your destination.

Hint: Use a piece of string and a globe. Then use the globe's key to change inches to miles.

_____

Find the average temperature for the month you'll be traveling.
Hint: Use an atlas.

_____

List the clothing you'll pack.

_____

Find out which unit of money is used in the country you'll visit.

Hint: Look for "Money" in the encyclopedia article about the country you're studying.

_____

Find out what time it is at your destination if your flight leaves at 1 P.M.

Hint: Use the world time zones chart in an encyclopedia.

_____

List three things a native from the country you're visiting could share with you about his or her country. Use the back if you need more space.

1. _____

2. _____

3. _____

Bonus Box: What souvenir could you bring back from your trip? On the back of this sheet, write a paragraph describing it and explaining why you bought it.

Note to the teacher: Provide an atlas, a globe, string, scissors, a ruler, and a set of encyclopedias for students' use.

On a Roll With Social Studies!

Creative Activities for Teaching Social Studies Skills

Geography Bingo

Skill: Identifying geographic locations

Watch students' geography knowledge soar with this versatile game of bingo! To prepare, number the countries on a blank map of the continent you're currently studying. Include bodies of water and islands so that the total number is a multiple of five. Provide each student with a copy of the map. Then have him color each numbered location, making sure to use each color only five times (see the example).

Next, play a few practice rounds by calling out a location's name and its number. Have each student cover the place with a small scrap of white paper. When a student has covered five sections of the same color, he calls "Bingo!" Check by having the student state each number and its geographic name. Continue playing until several students win. Then have students clear their maps to begin a new game. This time, call out only the geographic names. Adapt this game to help students learn states and capitals or countries and their capitals.

Denise Fischer
Rio del Mar School
Aptos, CA

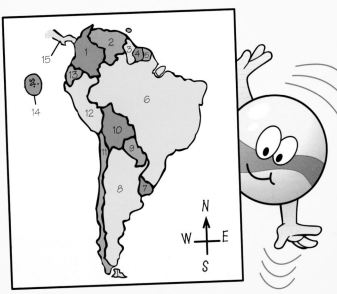

Taxation Without Representation!

Skill: Critical thinking

What was taxation without representation *really* like? Try this simulation to help your students relate to an emotional event in our nation's history. Before studying the American Revolution, share with your students an official-looking (but fake!) letter stating that in one week the school lunch price will increase by one dollar. Tell students that you have no control over the situation; then ask how they feel about it. Students will likely get fired up and come up with ideas on how to fight the decision. Remind them they are *only* children; then the ideas will really start to fly! List their suggestions on the board and discuss the merit of each one. Once students have come up with several ideas, reveal that the letter isn't real. Further explain that you wanted to give them a better understanding of how the colonists felt when they learned they were going to be taxed. As a follow-up, have students design posters encouraging the colonists to stand up and fight for their rights.

Aimee Dunn
Fairfield South Elementary
Fairfield, OH

State Alphabet Book

Skills: Creative thinking, art

These alphabet books are the perfect culminating activity when studying your state (or a U.S. region or a country). First, have each student list a word or phrase that begins with each letter of the alphabet and that is associated with or describes your state. Then, as a class, vote on the word for each letter that best represents your state. Next, divide students into groups and assign each group several letters and words. For each letter, have the group create a page for its word that includes a few descriptive sentences and an illustration. After all the pages are complete, bind them together to make "[Your state's] Alphabet Book."

Cathy Ogg
Happy Valley Elementary
Elizabethton, TN

C ountry Music

Country music is a major industry and tourist attraction in Tennessee.

Parade of Historical Personalities

Skills: Research, writing a report

Make the famous people of any historical period come to life with this giant-sized project! Have each student select a historical figure from the time period you're studying; then have her research her person and write a brief report. Next, divide students into pairs. Give each pair two large sheets of white bulletin board paper. Instruct each student to trace her partner's body on a sheet of paper. Have students cut out their tracings. Then have them research the clothing of the time period and decorate their tracings to look like the people they have researched. Hang the completed cutouts and reports in a hallway to create a parade of historical personalities.

Sharon Seybold
Loring Flemming Elementary
Blackwood, NJ

Patrick Henry

Answer Keys

Page 31
Answers will vary. Accept all reasonable answers.

American industry grew because…
  there were more railroads
  there were lots of new inventions
  America had lots of raw materials
  America had lots of workers
  there were improved machines
  the government didn't have many restrictions on industry

Because of the Industrial Revolution…
  immigrants came to America
  cities grew larger
  women and children were often hired to work in factories
  more machines were used to make goods
  the use of machines made work more boring
  some workers lost their jobs to machines
  more goods were produced
  prices of goods were lower
  some people became very wealthy while the workers remained poor
  some people worked and lived in very harsh conditions
  some people had better living conditions
  companies became so large that many workers didn't see the
    company owners very much
  workers became dissatisfied with poor working conditions and began
    to try to change these conditions

Bonus Box: Answers will vary.

Page 46
United States
Divided into 50 states and the District of Columbia
One official language: English
Fourth largest country in the world in area
President is head of government
Legislative branch is the Congress
Legislative branch has a Senate and a House of Representatives
Senators elected to six-year terms
Began as British colonies
Population more than 270 million
Type of government: federal republic
National capital: Washington, DC
National anthem: "The Star-Spangled Banner"

Canada
Divided into ten provinces and three territories
Two official languages: English and French
Second largest country in the world in area
Prime minister is head of government
Legislative branch is the parliament
Federal parliament has a Senate and a House of Commons
Senators appointed for life (or until 75 years of age)
Population about 30 million
Type of government: confederation with parliamentary democracy
National capital: Ottawa
National anthem: "O Canada"
Began as a French colony

Both
Basic unit of money: dollar
Mining products: petroleum, natural gas, coal
Borders these oceans: Arctic, Atlantic, and Pacific
Known as a nation of immigrants
Railways helped westward expansion
Has six time zones

Page 48
Answers related to population figures are based on the 2001 census. Students' answers to the discussion questions may vary. Accept all reasonable responses.

1.

NUNAVUT TERR.
NORTHWEST TERR.
YUKON TERR.
SASKATCHEWAN
ALBERTA
BRITISH COLUMBIA
MANITOBA

NEWFOUNDLAND
QUEBEC
PRINCE EDWARD ISLAND
NEW BRUNSWICK
NOVA SCOTIA
ONTARIO

2. red: Ontario, Quebec
   blue: Alberta, British Columbia, Manitoba
   green: New Brunswick, Newfoundland, Nova Scotia, Prince
     Edward Island, Saskatchewan
   yellow: Northwest Territories, Nunavut Territory, Yukon Territory

3. These areas have extremely cold temperatures and harsh terrains.

4. Quebec and Ontario: 18,647,525 people
   Canada's remaining areas: 11,359,569 people
   More than half of Canada's population lives in the two provinces of
     Quebec and Ontario.

5. Total population of Canada: 30,007,094 people

6. Most of Canada's population lives within 100 miles of its southern
   border because the climate is better there.

Bonus Box:

Ontario	11,410,046	New Brunswick	729,498
Quebec	7,237,479	Newfoundland	512,930
British Columbia	3,907,738	Prince Edward Island	135,294
Alberta	2,974,807	Northwest Territories	37,360
Manitoba	1,119,583	Yukon Territory	28,674
Saskatchewan	978,933	Nunavut Territory	26,745
Nova Scotia	908,007		

Page 55
Maya
Empire centered in southern Mexico and Central America
Worshipped gods and goddesses
Ate cornmeal pancakes
Had no central form of government
Were conquered by the Spanish

Aztec
Empire centered in Mexico
Worshipped gods and goddesses
Ate cornmeal pancakes
Had their capital at the city of Tenochtitlán
Were conquered by the Spanish

Inca
Empire centered in Andes highlands
Worshipped gods and goddesses
Used llamas to carry their goods
Spoke a language called *Quechua*
Were conquered by the Spanish

Page 56
Nouns: boards, Europe, masks, writing, animals, dice, lake, fireplace
Verbs: understood, was, carried, raised, built, is
Adjectives: fancy, valuable, married, huge, more
Adverbs: dutifully, patiently, still
Pronouns: their, them, they

Bonus Box: Answers may vary. Suggested answers are buildings, artwork, tools, bones, and pottery.

Page 63

Park		Location
9 =	Yosemite	CA
7 =	Rocky Mountain	CO
11 =	Denali	AK
2 =	Grand Canyon	AZ
10 =	Zion	UT
6 =	Olympic	WA
12 =	Hawaii Volcanoes	HI
1 =	Acadia	ME
8 =	Yellowstone	WY, MT, ID
3 =	Grand Teton	WY
5 =	Mammoth Cave	KY
4 =	Great Smoky Mountains	NC, TN
14 =	Badlands	SD
13 =	Isle Royale	MI

Regions:
Blue: MD, DE, NJ, PA, NY, CT, RI, MA, VT, NH, ME
Green: VA, WV, KY, TN, AR, LA, MS, AL, GA, FL, SC, NC
Yellow: ND, SD, NE, KS, MN, IA, MO, WI, MI, IL, IN, OH
Orange: AZ, NM, TX, OK
Red: CA, NV, UT, CO, WY, ID, OR, WA, MT, AK, HI

Page 75

Part 1
1. Pacific Ocean
2. Atlantic Ocean
3. Gulf of Mexico
4. Sierra Nevada
5. Cascade Range
6. Rocky Mountains
7. Appalachian Mountains
8. Great Lakes
9. Mississippi River
10. Alaska Range

Part 2

Quillayute, WA—blue
Astoria, OR—blue
Bishop, CA—brown
Bakersfield, CA—brown
Blue Canyon, CA—orange
Las Vegas, NV—brown
Yuma, AZ—brown and red
Phoenix, AZ—brown
International Falls, MN—yellow
Duluth, MN—yellow
Marquette, MI—orange and yellow

Sault Ste. Marie, MI—orange
   and yellow
Mobile, AL—blue
Pensacola, FL—blue
Tallahassee, FL—blue
Key West, FL—red
Fort Myers, FL—red
Miami, FL—red
West Palm Beach, FL—red
Syracuse, NY—orange
Caribou, ME—orange and yellow

Part 3
Answers may vary. Accept all reasonable responses.
1. Because California is one of the largest states, it has a wide variety of climates and land regions of different elevations. The state includes several mountain ranges, valleys of rich farmland, and desert areas.
2. Las Vegas doesn't receive much rain. Clouds that move eastward from the Pacific Ocean lose most of their moisture in California as they rise above the Sierra Nevada.
3. They are all near large bodies of water.
4. The hottest cities are located nearer to the equator (at lower latitudes) than the coldest cities. The coldest cities are farther away from the equator (at higher latitudes) than the hottest cities.

Page 80

Answers will vary depending on the symbols that each student chooses. Features should be drawn in the approximate locations shown.

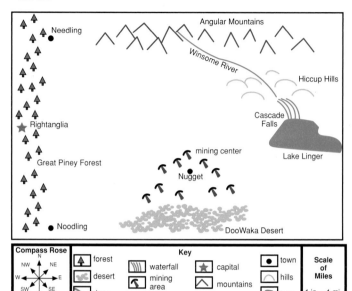

Bonus Box: Answers will vary.

Page 102

Causes of World War I: a, e, g, k, o, p
Reasons USA Entered War: b, f
Results of World War I: c, d, h, i, j, l, m, n

Page 103

Part 1:
1. World War I ends.
2. Americans buy huge amounts of goods.
3. Factories increase production of goods.
4. Demand for products falls because people can't afford to keep purchasing them.
5. Warehouses and stores become full of products that go unsold.
6. People buy stock on credit to try to make more money.
7. Stock prices drop drastically. Many investors lose all of their money.
8. Many banks and businesses fail. Many people lose their jobs.
9. The Great Depression begins.
10. President Franklin D. Roosevelt proposes New Deal programs to end the depression.

Part 2: Answers will vary.